Poetry of Moray

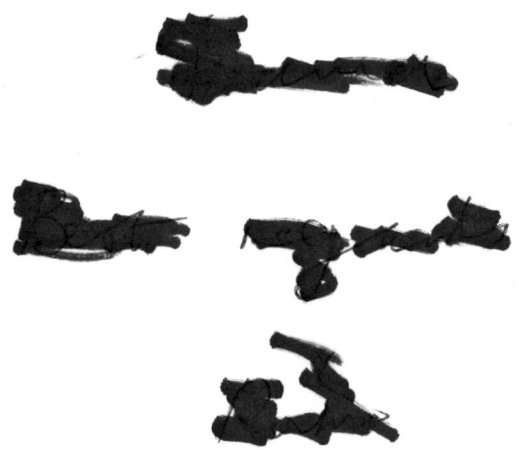

'this delectable plain of Moray, entitled the Granary of Scotland...being distinguished by equality of surface, fertility of soil, and amenity of climate.'

Beriah Botfield, *Tour of the Highlands*, 1829

Poetry of Moray

1448 – 1984

Editor
Richard Bennett

First Published 2021

© of all poetry is that of copyright holders, where copyright exists. Every effort has been made to trace the copyright holders and obtain permission to reproduce this material. Please get in touch using the email below for any enquiries about rights.
© introduction Richard Bennett

Richard Bennett has asserted his moral rights under the Copyright, Designs and Patents Act 1988 to be identified as the author of his section of this work.

All rights reserved. No part of this publication may be reproduced or transmitted in any form or by any means, electronic, or mechanical, including photocopying, recording, or any information storage or retrieval system, without prior permission in writing from the publishers.

Spey Publishing Ltd, **Kemp House, 160 City Road, London, United Kingdom, EC1V 2NX** www.speybooks.co.uk   john@speybooks.co.uk   fb.me/speybooks
A CIP catalogue record for this title is available from the British Library.
ISBN 9781916359420

1 2 3 4 5 6 7 8 9 10

Designed and set by Speybooks
Printed and bound in the UK by Clays Ltd, Elcograf S.p.A.
Cover illustration: Joey Sim
Printed on FSC paper

'From Findhorn east to Findlater the well-loved beaches run,
By Cummingstown and Covesea – grey, golden, rose, and dun;
And the alien land shall fade away; afar mine eyes shall see
The Moray Firth and the Ross-shire hills and the days
　that used to be.'

Hilton Brown, *Moray Beaches,* 1930

Contents

Introduction	9
Acknowledgements	21
Richard Holland (died in or after 1483)	23
Robert Alves (1745 – 1794)	31
Mrs Grant of Carron (1745 – 1828)	35
James Cock (1752 – c.1824)	37
Robert Jamieson (1772 – 1844)	42
John Grant (c. 1790 – c.1840)	47
John Milne of Glenlivat (1792 – 1871)	51
William Hay (1794 – 1854)	56
James Murdoch – 'Cutler Jamie' (1806 – 1872)	68
William Hay Leith Tester - 'La Teste' (1829 – 1892)	72
Frank Sutherland – 'Uncle Peter' (1837–1920)	81
Lady Middleton (1847 – 1922)	91
William Donaldson (1847 – 1876)	96
James Simpson (1850 – death unknown)	99

James McQueen (1852 – 1928)	104
Reverend John Wellwood (1853 – 1919)	108
David J Mackenzie (1855 – 1925)	112
May C Dawson (1860 – 1947)	118
Mary Symon (1863 - 1938)	121
Nannie Katharin Wells (1875 – 1963)	132
JM Caie (1878 – 1949)	137
Andrew Young (1885–1971)	147
William J Grant (1886 – 1951)	152
George Riddler (1886 – died after 1937)	154
Hilton Brown (1890 – 1971)	157
Ella Gilbert (1890 – 1975)	164
Margaret Winefride Simpson (1893 – 1972)	173
Lilianne Grant Rich (1910 –1997)	177
Jessie Kesson (1916 – 1994)	180
Bibliography	187
Glossary	190
Selected Glossary for *The Buke of the Howlat*	196

Introduction

At a meeting of the London Morayshire Club in the Guildhall Tavern, City of London, on 17th October, 1930, the annual 'County' Lecture was delivered by Reverend Graham Warner, Assistant Minister of St Giles Church in Elgin. The lecture was entitled *The Muse of Morayland: Glimpses of Life and Works of Moray Poets*. It was later published as a booklet, by the *Elgin Courant and Courier*. The lecture gives samples of the work and touches on details of the lives of thirty-three poets who were born in, or who lived for some time, in Moray from the end of the eighteenth century to the 1920s.

Reverend Warner takes, as the geographical limits of 'Morayland', the 'old' county boundary, as it was before the re-organisation of local government in 1975 – from the Culbin Sands in the West to the Tynet Burn, that enters the sea between Spey Bay and Buckie in the East, and to Dulnain Bridge, two miles south of Grantown on Spey, and including the old parish of Cromdale, to the east of the Spey.

For the purposes of the present collection of poems, I have adopted the boundaries of the 'council area' of Moray as it is in 2020, which includes a significant portion of the former county of Banffshire, stretching from Cullen on the coast to the Cairngorms.

For many people throughout history, resident and visitor,

Moray has meant much more than an insignificant little triangle of territory in the far North. The word 'Morayland', indeed, suggests a realm, a people, an expansive landscape, rich in fame and story. It suggests feelings of pride and love like those expressed in the Preface to the first edition of *The Lintie o Moray* (1851) for 'the heath-covered hills, the oft-frequented streams', 'the classic haunts of happy boyhood's prime'.

'Moray' as a name for a stretch of the earth's surface, goes back long before the formation of counties. The ancient Province of Moray and the Bishopric encompassed the old shires of Moray and Nairn and large areas of Inverness-shire and Ross and Cromarty. The Province was very important in political, social, and religious terms, and the first poem represented in this collection, Richard Holland's *The Buke of the Howlat*, composed in the middle of the fifteenth century, is testimony to that importance. The poet, a highly educated cleric, creates an ornate poetic form, incorporating rhyme and alliteration, that suggests the existence of a sophisticated audience that could respond to the subtleties of form as well as to the poem's political and moral satire.

*

Apart from the inclusion of extracts from *The Buke of the Howlat*, the present collection offers a representative sample of some 250 years of the work of a wide range of poets. Authors range from the highly educated classical scholars of the late eighteenth and early nineteenth centuries to self-taught, itinerant beggars; from aristocratic ladies to educated men and women of the Victorian and Edwardian middle classes, who pursued their literary aspirations in smooth and polished verse.

Education has always been highly regarded in the North-East. From the early thirteenth century, religious establish-

Introduction

ments associated with the Cathedral in Elgin and the monasteries at Kinloss and Pluscarden were centres of learning. There was a university in Aberdeen. However, before the Education (Scotland) Act of 1872, schooling opportunities throughout the country were limited. Elgin Academy, which opened in 1801, and the Grammar School that preceded it provided education only for the sons of men in the area who could afford to pay for it. It was not uncommon for a boy in a country area to attend school for only a few weeks in the quieter winter months over a year or two, as work permitted.

Poets such as Robert Alves, Robert Jamieson, James Cock, Will Hay, James Murdoch, William Hay Leith Tester, Frank Sutherland, and James McQueen, who played his fiddle on the trains that served the Northern counties, as late as the 1920s, came from the lowest orders of society. A few – Alves, Jamieson, and Hay, for example – struck it lucky in acquiring education through a patron or patrons. Others were almost entirely self-educated.

The near absence of women in the first half of this anthology – only Elizabeth Grant of Carron and Lady Middleton appear – may reflect the very limited opportunities for education available to girls outside the privileged classes. We do know that, throughout the eighteenth and nineteenth centuries, women played key roles in conserving and transmitting the ballad and folksong oral traditions of the North-East of Scotland. It was, however, the twentieth century before prejudices diminished sufficiently to enable women to publish their own work and earn money from it.

*

From the eighteenth century, Moray was an aspirational society with a growing appetite for education in formal and informal contexts. Improvements took place. Farms got bigger.

Planned towns and villages sprang up. Elgin and Forres re-invented themselves as modern 'county' towns. Wealth accrued.

Writing poetry is an aspirational activity. Its purpose is to share thoughts, feelings, ideas, stories, by using – according to the great poets – 'the best words in the best order' 'to please, move, and transport'. In the nineteenth century, two monthly literary magazines were produced in Elgin. *The Elgin Literary Magazine*, was launched in 1829 by James Grant of the *Elgin Courier*, brother of the author of *The Penny Wedding*. Most poems and articles were written by Grant, others by Will Hay (later the dominant voice in *The Lintie o Moray*). The remainder were submitted by post. On these, Grant delivered judgement: 'BA should have added the fourth letter of the alphabet, and then his signature would have appropriately characterised the quality of his verses'; 'we suspect BT of plagiarism. Is not our suspicion correct?' In 1876, *The Grey Friar, a monthly magazine of Literature and Art*, printed by James Watson, bookseller in Elgin, was published by David J Mackenzie, a young man of barely twenty with a distinguished legal and literary career ahead of him. Mackenzie contributed well over half the articles and poems. Articles ranged from elaborate, tongue-in-cheek, fictional pastiches with an 'antique' flavour, to articles on the novels of George Eliot, local antiquities, and the Lepidoptera of Moray.

Each of these ambitious literary projects lasted about a year. However, the fact is that, in Victorian times, poetry was a popular form of entertainment. Following the repeal of stamp duties in 1853, newspapers came within the reach of many more people, and were an important part of the week – something to look forward to, to read and re-read and to pass on. By the middle of the century, poems were a common feature of the weekly press in Scotland. Every week, newspapers like the *Elgin Courant and Courier* and the *Moray and Nairn Express*

Introduction

(later the *Northern Scot*) carried one or two poems. Occasionally, these were poems picked up from other publications but, often, they were originals submitted by local men – in Moray, almost always by men – in order to make a little money.

The establishment of the Dundee-based *People's Journal* in 1858 played an important part in raising the profile of poetry among working people. The paper offered prizes for poetry written by readers. Newspapers were shared, read in workplaces, in communal reading rooms and libraries, and sent by post to relatives in the South or in the Colonies. It is probably true to say that, in the second half of the nineteenth century, poetry played a significantly larger part in the culture of everyday life of working people than it does today. Testimony to the popularity of poetry is the remarkable achievement of David Herschell Edwards, editor of the *Brechin Advertiser*, in publishing, between 1880 and 1897, fifteen volumes under the title *Modern Scottish Poets*. These volumes carried the work of about one thousand poets.

Poems of this period tended to be simple and conservative – often clichéd – in form and meaning. Robert Burns – in his use of Scots and in his metrical forms and in his focus on the lives of ordinary people – was a model for aspiring working-class poets. Poets might secure a few pence weekly by submitting pieces to the papers, but they also had ideas of building a subscription list for possible future publication in broadsheet, pamphlet, or book form.

By the end of the first quarter of the twentieth century, the voices of the 'Scottish Renaissance', led by Hugh MacDiarmid, were loud in their disdain for the work of these 'popular' poets. Maurice Lindsay wrote in 1946,

> 'the art of poetry reached its nadir in Scotland in the nineteenth century where minor vernacular poets out-

did each other in alternate laments and hiccoughs', *[producing]* 'unskilled and inconsequential pastiche.'

Reverend Warner, in *The Muse in Morayland*, while democratic in his selection and including 'newspaper poets', is similarly dismissive. He calls them 'Rhymers' and suggests that some wrote,

'with a desire to show a certain superiority over the rest of mankind', *[while]* 'others wrote verses – well! heaven only knows why they did write verses'.

These poets were self-taught, working men. Their poems might be humorous or playful or radical, in political terms; they might be sentimental or elegiac or address a social problem or be dedicated to a particular person who might put a little money the poet's way. Importantly, their work is worthy of study and should be read and judged on its own terms, not by the aesthetic values of a progressive literary movement. Often their work dealt with aspects of the lives of ordinary working people in thoughtful and sympathetic ways. Their poems celebrated the stories, the characters, the institutions, the landscape, the traditions of the homeland. Games were played: in one *Elgin Courier* in 1865, La Teste publishes an *Epitaph on the death of Cutler Jamie*; the following week, the paper carries an elegy by Cutler Jamie on the passing of La Teste. Both poems refer to the heavy drinking culture of which both men were part. The popularity of these poems suggests a community of readers that understood the writer's intentions and aspirations. These are poems of the people, the place, and the time, but they are not necessarily parochial. In 1865, for example, La Teste published *Notes from the Bird*. He imagines himself as the Dove, flying from the Ark in Scotland to bring

Introduction

peace in the American Civil War. On arriving exhausted, the birds of Virginia offer the Dove a drink:

> 'But they brought me a skull that was brimming full
> With the blood of last night's slaughter.'

After describing the Confederate vultures feeding on that 'dainty dish, the Yankee flesh', he offers the following prayer:

> 'Let the black and white as brothers unite,
> The young and the fair and the hoary;
> Let a halo of love from thy mansion above
> Encircle the earth with its glory.'

In the same volume he publishes *Lossie*:

> 'Oe'r rugged crags an pebbles glossy,
> Through verdant woods wi hillsides mossy,
> Meanders gentle, gurgling Lossie,
> Dear to my heart;
> The bonniest stream in aa Ecossais
> I swear thou art.'

The obituarist of La Teste in the *Northern Scot* of 12 March, 1892, writes:

> 'Be it remembered, while dealing with this subject, that for many years La Teste contrived, or at any rate attempted, to earn a living by his poetry, and often, in order to attain this laudable object, he was compelled to resort to strange expedients – in plain parlance, to sell the products of his muse in the readiest market. Where he failed to dispose of a book, he would snatch

up a pen, or fumble in his pockets for a pencil, and forthwith scribble down verses, to show his facility or to secure his end. These he afterwards incorporated in his collections. They were his, and why should they not be honoured; the course grain could go with the fine and help to fill the granary.'

In a small community – Elgin, for example, had a population of about 5000 in the mid-nineteenth century – poets appearing regularly in the press became celebrities. 'Poets' Corner' in the weekly newspaper was sought out, passed around, criticised, appreciated. The anonymous author of the biographical memoir published in the *Songs and Poems of the late John Milne of Glenlivat* (1871) points to the appeal of such writers:

'While his rugged numbers and unceremonious sarcasms gave immense satisfaction to his patrons of the farm-servant class, and drew many a copper from their pockets, he took a general interest in all subjects, political, religious, and social. Left to his own impulses and guided by his own feelings, his sympathies were always with the suffering and the struggling, with honest poverty and true merit. And, in short, if there was a grievance to redress – national, local or personal – his pen was always ready.'

*

Of the poets born after 1850, the majority came from an educated, professional background and earned their livings as minister, lawyer, journalist, university lecturer, civil servant, Colonial officer. Women poets, too, became prominent, as opportunities for education at a higher level became availa-

Introduction

ble for women. The work of those writing at the end of the nineteenth and in the first decades of the twentieth century is polished in form and language and tended to be published in books compiled over a few years, with introductions written by distinguished men of letters – Compton Mackenzie, Professor Sir Herbert Grierson, John Geddie and J Ramsay Macdonald – the Prime Minister, no less. Among these are writers of high international standing in Andrew Young and Jessie Kesson.

*

About three quarters of the poems printed here are written in Scots. The language varies according to the situation presented and the voice chosen. It is clear that, for many, the use of Scots is a key element in the creative process, enabling the expression of nuanced meanings that are not possible in English. In the best work, the Doric language is employed with such vigour, humour, and assurance, in the creation of character, situation and poetic effect as to make readers see the medium as an important part of the message.

From 1872, through the first half of the twentieth century, demotic Scots, the language of the people, was under serious threat. On the one hand it was being beaten out of children in schools, on the other, its status was being attacked by Hugh MacDiarmid and others, as hopelessly debased and corrupt and completely unsuitable for a national literary form. MacDiarmid, in his early lyrics in collections such as *Sangshaw* (1925) and *Penny Wheep* (1926), created a vibrant 'new Scots', drawing from a range of dialects and with strong links to the Scots of the fifteenth and sixteenth centuries. MacDiarmid's Scots was critically important in the developments in Scottish poetry and in prose that were taking place in the 1920s and

1930s, but it was a literary medium, quite distinct from the words and idioms used in the speech of ordinary people.

On the other hand, Mary Symon of Pittyvaich, while being very critical of some of the vapid, mawkish stuff presented as vernacular poetry in her day, is firmly committed to using the language of the glens of Upper Banffshire. Another poet in this collection who makes powerful and genuinely creative use of the 'spik' of his upbringing is JM Caie of the Enzie. For these and others here, the use of the local language is key to asserting the identity of their place and their folk.

*

When the notion of this anthology became firm, and I began, under the guidance of Reverend Graham Warner's booklet, to look back and forwards over the years for poets and poems, I was immensely gratified by the range, the diversity, and the quality of what I found. Not just from the names I knew – Jamieson, Symon, Young, Kesson – but from those I'd never heard of – Milne, La Teste, Wellwood, Wells. What I learned of the remarkable lives of many of the poets strengthened my commitment to complete the task.

I have tried to select the 'best' of an author's work and I have also chosen poems that are representative of the social and literary culture of their particular time and place. The collection includes responses to landscape and nature, expressions of love and loss, and representations of aspects of local life. There are vivid accounts of the desperate hardships to be found on the streets of the towns and of the relentless grind of farm work. There is a number of poems about Moray, the homeland. In his introduction to Margaret Winefride Simpson's *Day's End* (1924), Compton Mackenzie, casting a sidelong glance at Miss Simpson herself, writes, 'I want to hear

Introduction

no more songs of exile, because I dread the easy outlet they provide for a barren sentimentality'. A number of poems in this collection do dwell on the importance of memory – on Moray, as 'a land of lost content'. I trust that only a little may be found of what Mary Symon calls 'walshach an dweeble'.

I have, to some small extent, regularised the varied orthography of the texts presented here. In particular, I have removed the recurring apostrophe that suggests that words in the Scots tongue are, somehow, corruptions of Standard English words. We should be clear: 'aa' and 'aul' and 'gyaun' and 'tak' are Scots words, our words, and require no apology.

My hope is that readers will use their own resources and the bibliographies published at the end of this book, to explore and seek out more of the riches to be found in Moray's poetic heritage.

Acknowledgements

I would like to thank the staff of Moray Local Heritage Service, based in Elgin Library; the staff of Special Collections at the Sir Duncan Rice Library of the University of Aberdeen; and the staff of the National Library of Scotland. Without the assistance of these amazing groups of public servants, I could not have put the anthology together.

Profound thanks to The Doric Board. Their financial support will enable me to provide copies of the book free of charge to every school and to every Care Home in Moray.

I am very grateful to Professor Alison Lumsden of the University of Aberdeen, to Dr Eilidh Whiteford, to Dr David Northcroft, and to the staff of the Elphinstone Institute for their advice and encouragement; and to Heather Gibson for her proof-reading expertise. I am grateful, too, to Ruth Lowbury, grand-daughter of Andrew Young, for putting me right on aspects of her grandfather's life and career.

I must also thank my family, in particular, John, for his comprehensive publishing skills; Joey, for her splendid cover; Molly, for her precise and prompt word-processing; and Susan, for her unstinting support in the production of this book.

'Ploughing in Mist', 'Suilven', 'Mountain View', 'Culbin Sands', 'Passing the Graveyard', and 'Hard Frost', by Andrew Young (*Selected Poems*, 1998) are reprinted here by kind permission of Carcanet Press Limited, Manchester, UK.

'Blaeberry Wood', 'A Scarlet Goon', 'Fir Wud'. 'The Spell Binders', by Jessie Kesson are reprinted here by kind permission of the Kesson family and Johnson and Alcock Limited, 74-79 Great Russell Street, London.

All efforts have been made to contact copyright holders. If you have any queries about copyright please contact john@speybooks.co.uk.

Richard Holland (died c.1483)

Richard Holland served as a priest in Caithness before coming to Moray. He was employed at Darnaway Castle, near Forres, in the household of the Earl of Moray, who, in a charter of 1450, referred to Holland as his secretary.

Holland composed *The Buke of the Howlat*, in about 1448, written, we are told in the final stanza, at Darnaway and dedicated to the Countess of Moray, Elizabeth Dunbar, who had brought the Earldom to her husband, Archibald Douglas.

The work is the earliest major poem of the Scottish alliterative revival. Its 1001 lines are arranged in 13-line stanzas. The poem is an animal fable, a comic allegory in which a young owl (howlat) who feels ugly in comparison with the other birds, appeals to the Pope (a peacock) to improve his appearance. The poem belongs to the same genre as Robert Henryson's *Morall Fabillis*, written a few years later. Answering the howlat's appeal, the Pope calls a council consisting of a hierarchy of clergy and the Emperor (an eagle). After a banquet is held with entertainers, the owl's request is granted. His new plumage is made up of a feather from each of the birds at the banquet, but, thus adorned, he becomes intolerably conceited; the other birds pluck their feathers back, and the howlat is left lamenting,

'That pryde nevir yit left
His feir but a fall.'

At the heart of the poem is a digression in the form of a defence of the Douglas dynasty, in particular, of their devotion to the Bruce cause. He tells the well-known story of how Sir James Douglas carried the heart of Robert the Bruce on an expedition to the Holy Land and, in so doing, lost his own life.

Holland's patron, Archibald Douglas was killed at the battle of Arkinholme in 1455. In 1467, Holland was a canon of Kirkwall Cathedral. Thereafter, he seems to have spent the rest of his life in political exile in England.

As a poet, he is, in Dunbar's *Lament for the Makaris,* placed in the highest company: 'Holland and Barbour he has berevit'.

The Buke of the Howlat makes, for the modern reader, an initially demanding, but ultimately satisfying read. The poem has had some attention in recent years with the publication in 2014 of a new scholarly edition and, in 2016, by two illustrated translations, for children, into modern Scots and English, of the 'bird fable' aspect of the poem. Here, we can offer no more than a few glimpses of the poem's form and language. There is a selected glossary for *The Buke of the Howlat* after the more general glossary at the end of this book.

The Buke of the Howlat
(On a fine May morning, the narrator walks by the Findhorn and glories in the beauty and the richness of the landscape.)

I.
In the myddist of May, at morne, as I ment,
Throwe myrth markit on mold, till a grene mead

Richard Holland (died c.1483)

The beames blythest of ble fro the son blent,
That all brichtened about the borderis on breid;
With alkyn herbes of air that war in erd lent
The fieldes flourisht and fret full of fairhed;
So soft was the season our Soverane doune sent,
Throw the agreable gift of his Godhed,
That all was amyable owr the air and the erth.
Thus, throw thir cliftis so cleir,
Withoutin fallowe or feir,
I raikit till ane River
That royally apperd.

II
This riche River doun ran, but resting or ruf,
Throwe ane forest on fold, that farly was fair;
All the brayis of the broom tbair branchis abuf,
And birdis blythest of ble on blossomes bair;
The land lowne was and lee, with lyking and luf,
And for to lende by that laik thocht me levar,
Becauss that thir harts in herdis couth huf,
Pransand and prunyeand, be pair and be pair.
Thus sat I in solace, sekerly and sure,
Content of the fair firth,
Mekle mair of the mirth,
Als blyth of the birth
That the ground bure.

III.
The birth that the ground bure was browdin on breidis,
With gorse gaye as the gold, and granes of grace,
Mendis and medicyne for men's all needs;
Helpe to hert and to hurt, heilfull it was.
Under the Cirkill solar thir savoruss seeds

War nourist by dame Natur, that noble mistress;
Bot all their names to nevyn as now it nocht need is
It war prolixt and lang, and lengthing of space,
And I haue meikle mattir in metre to gloss
Of anothir sentence,
And waike is my eloquence;
Tharfor in haste will I hence
To the purposs.

(He hears an owl lamenting the shame he feels for his appearance. The owl determines to appeal to the Pope to 'reforme [his] foul face'.)

V.
He grat grysly grym, and gaif a gret yowle,
Cheuerand and chydand with churliche cheir.
'Quhy is my face' quoth the fowl, 'fashionit so foule,
My forme and my fethers unfrely, but feir?
My neb is netherit as a nok, I am bot ane Owle;
Against nature in the nicht I walk in to weir;
I dare do nocht on the day, but droupe as a dovle,
Nocht for schame of my schape in pert till appeir.
Thus all thir fowlis, for my filth, has me at feid,
That be I seyne in thair sicht,
To luke out on day licht,
Sum will me doulfully dicht,
Sum dyng me to deid.

VI.
Sum bird will bay at my beike, and some will me byte,
Sum skripe me with scorne, sum skrym at myn ee;
I see by my schadowe my schape has the wyte.
Quhom sall I blame in this breath, a bysyn that I be?

Richard Holland (died c.1483)

Is nane bot dame Natur, I bid nocht to nyte,
To accuse of this caise, in case that I dee;
Bot quha sall mak me ane mendis of hir worth a myte,
That thus has maid on the mold ane monstour of me?
I will appele to the Pope, and pass till him plane;
For happin that his halyness
Thro prayer may purchase
To reforme my foul face,
And than war I fane.

(The Parliament of Fowls is called, the birds appearing as different ranks of churchmen.)

XIV.
Yet endurand the daye to that deir drewe,
Swannis suowchand full swyth, sweetest of swar,
In white rocatis arrayd; as I richt knewe
That they were bishops blesst, I was the blyther;
Stable and steidfast, tender and trewe,
Off fewe words, full wyiseand worthy thai war.
Thar was Pyots and Partriks and Plovers ynewe,
As abbots of all orders that honorable are;
The Sea Mawis war monks, the blak and the whyte,
The Goule was a gryntar.
The Suerthbak a sellerar,
The Scarth a fische fangar,
And that a perfyte.

XV.
Perfectly the Pikmawis, as for priors,
With thar party habits present tham thar;
Herons contemplative, clene charterours,
With toppit hoodis on hed, and clothing of hair.

Ay sorowfull and sad at evin sang and houris,
Was neuer leid saw thaim lauch, bot droopan and dar;
All kind canonis eik of vther orders,
All maner of religioun, the less and the mair;
Cryand Crawis and Cais, that crave the corne.
War pure freris forthward,
That, with the leif of the laird,
Will cum to the corne yeard
At evyn and at morn.

(At the heart of the poem, the poet digresses from the tale of the birds to pay lavish tribute, by means of a discussion of heraldry, to his patrons, the Douglas family.)

XXXI.
Of the douchty Dowglass to dyte I me dress;
Thar armes of ancestry honorable ay,
Quhilk oft blythit the Bruce in his distress,
Tharfor he blessit that bluid bold in assay.
Reid the writ of thar werk, to your witness;
Furth on my matir to muse I mufe as I may.
The said persevantis gyde was grathit, I gess,
Brusit with ane grene tre, gudly and gay,
That bure branchis on breid blythest of hewe;
On ilk beugh till embrace,
Writtin in a bill was,
O Dowglass, O Dowglass,
Tender and trewe!

(The Court continues to assemble. The birds have a feast, the fun grows fast and furious; a bard arrives from Ireland who addresses the gathering in mock-Gaelic. A fight breaks out between a teuchat and a gowk.)

Richard Holland (died c.1483)

LXII.
Sa come the Ruke with a rerd and a rane roch,
A bard owt of Irland with Banachadee!
Said: Gluntow guk dynyd dach hala mischy doch;
Raike hir a rug of the rost, or scho sall ryive the.
Mich macmory ach mach mometir moch loch;
Set hir doune, gif hir drink; quhat Dele aylis the?
O Deremyne, O Donnall, O Dochardy droch;
Thir ar his Irland kingis of the Irischerye:
O Knewlyn, O Conochor, O Gregre Makgrane;
The Schenachy, the Clarschach,
The Ben schene, the Ballach,
The Crekery, the Corach,
Scho kennis thaim ilkane.

(Dame Nature is called. Each bird donates a feather to the Howlat, who becomes intolerably conceited. Nature intervenes again, the birds retrieve their feathers and fly off home. The Howlat has learned its lesson. The narrator finishes as follows:)

LXXVII.
Thus for ane Dow of Dunbar drew I this Dyte,
Dowit with ane Dowglass, and boith war thai dowis;
In the forest forsaid, frely parfyte,
Of Terneway, tendir and tryde, quho so trast trowis.
War my wit as my will, than suld I wele wryte;
Bot gif I lak in my leid, that nocht till allow is,
Ye wyse, for your worschipe, wryth me no wyte.
Now blyth ws the blist barne, that all berne bowis;
He len ws lyking and lyf euerlestand!
In mirthfull moneth of May,

In myddis of Murraye,
Thus on a tyme be Ternway,
Happinnit Holland.

Robert Alves (1745 - 1794)

Robert Alves was born, one of a large family, in Elgin on December 11, 1745. He was a promising student at the Elgin Grammar School and won the highest bursary of his year and a place at Marischal College, Aberdeen. His poetry gained him the admiration and friendship of Professor James Beattie, author of *The Minstrel*.

He trained for the ministry and, after leaving Aberdeen, Alves was master of the parish school in Deskford, near Cullen, before being offered a living in the Church of Scotland. However, he turned down this offer and became, instead, Rector of the Banff Grammar School, a post he held from 1773 until 1779. Alves was a hopeless schoolteacher. He fancied himself, first and foremost, as a poet and scholar, but had poor discipline, and a tendency to bouts of excessive drinking. He was 'removed' from his post. The story is that he was ardently pursuing a lady, the 'Delia' of his poems and, when he finally had to accept her rejection, he moved to Edinburgh, where, for the rest of his life, Alves worked as a tutor, teaching the classics and several modern languages, including Italian, French, Spanish, and Portuguese; occasionally translating and compiling for Edinburgh booksellers; and working on his *Sketches of the History of Literature*. In this last ambitious and innovative project, Alves, 'intended to exhibit a critical review of literature from the earliest times; a subject pregnant both with instruction and entertainment' and offering 'a distinct view of ancient and modern learning, with a just estimation of most writers, whether in philosophy, poetry, history, or oratory'.

In 1782, he published his *Poems*, and in 1789, *Edinburgh, a Poem in Two Parts*, which describes the topography and social aspects of the capital, together with the *Weeping Bard*, in which he laments, in sixteen tear-sodden Cantos, 'a childish, foolish life, at best'. The poems are classically inspired in form, language, and reference. In the *Annals of Elgin* (1879), Robert Young writes,

'In these works, much genius is not to be discovered; but they bear the impression of a cultivated mind and much poetic susceptibility'.

Alves died suddenly in Edinburgh on June 1, 1794. His *Sketches of the History of Literature* was published after his death. This book, clumsy and flawed as it is, shows insight, promotes Scottish authors, and deserves credit as one of the very first attempts at a comprehensive history of literature.

Time: an Elegy Written near the Ruins of Elgin Cathedral

Part 1
'Twas at the sober hour of closing day,
When night fast-falling wraps the world in shade,
Musing I bent my solitary way,
For yon pale mansions of the silent Dead.

Robert Alves (1745 – 1794)

Hard by, yon ancient pile, with ivy crown'd,
(Memorial sad of Time's resistless sway),
Here towers to heaven, there cumbers all the ground,
With vast unwieldy heaps of old decay.

To solemn thought invites the solemn scene,
The earth wide-hush'd , and heaven's refulgent fires;
And Cynthia, riding in her car serene,
Affections gentle as herself inspires

When thus the Muse: 'Be scenes like these thy theme,
Man's life how vain, his joys, his labours all!' –
I heard, and felt the soft-inspiring flame,
And wept to see the mouldering columns fall …

Yet to console the lots there still remain
Works blest of Genius, works of noblest lay;
Homer's bold fire, and Virgil's lofty strain,
Tibullus' weeping muse, and Horace gay …

The Smiles and Loves once fled, are ever fled;
And fled each blithesome hour that erst had shone,
When jocund Fancy, like some buxom maid,
Before them danc'd, and led them sporting on.

These are Time's triumphs; while his black compeer,
Death, writhes his ghastly visage to a smile;
And, grimly-pleas'd, surveys the conquer'd year,
Exulting in the partner of his toil.

To Delia

My charmer, hear my pensive strain,
From heart more pensive still;

That heart that aye must thine remain,
Now left to weep at will.

As pity bids the gentle dove
To love and peace incline:
Such pity, tenderness, and love,
Melt down that heart of thine.

And sure no other mortal Fair,
No goddess of the sky,
Could more of love or pity bear,
In melting air or eye.

Thy voice does o'er my bosom steal,
Like music soft and slow;
As zephyrs o'er the lilied vale
Complain, and gently blow.

Thy looks and smiles, whene'er we meet,
Reward an age of care;
Could they alone to me seem sweet,
How boundless blest I were.

Fair are thine eyes, of heavenly blue,
Dear emblems of thy mind!
O would my Delia prove but true,
As these declare her kind!

Mrs Grant of Carron (1745 – 1828)

Elizabeth Grant was born near Aberlour. She was married, about 1765, to her cousin, Captain James Grant of Carron. They had five sons. Her husband died in 1790. Mrs Grant later married Dr James Thomas Murray and moved to Bath where she died in 1828, aged eighty-two.

Her reputation as a poet and songwriter rests exclusively on *Roy's Wife of Aldivalloch*. The song is a young man's lament for his lost love who marries an older man. Aldivalloch is a farm in the Upper Cabrach. John Roy of Aldivalloch, married a young bride, Isabel Stewart, in 1727. She ran off with a lover and was brought back after a chase over the Braes of Balloch. Or so the story goes. A song based on the story may have existed in the oral tradition before Mrs Grant published her version. Such was often the way with folksong.

Mrs Grant's version of *Roy's Wife* was very popular. Burns admired it and used the air for his own song, *Rob the Ranter*.

Roy's Wife of Aldivalloch
Roy's wife of Aldivalloch,
Roy's wife of Aldivalloch,
Wat ye how she cheated me,
As I came oer the braes of Balloch?

She vow'd, she swore she wad be mine;
She said she loed me best of onie;
But O the fickle, faithless quean,
She's ta'en the carle and left her Johnnie!
Roy's wife of Aldivalloch etc.

O she was a canty quean,
And weel could dance the Highland walloch;
How happy I had she been mine,
Or I been Roy of Aldivalloch,
Roy's wife of Aldivalloch etc

Her hair sae fair, her e'en sae clear,
Her wee bit mou sae sweet and bonnie,
To me she ever will be dear,
Tho she's forever left her Johnnie.
Roy's wife of Aldivalloch,
Roy's wife of Aldivalloch,
Wat ye how she cheated me,
As I came oer the braes of Balloch?

James Cock (1752 – c.1824)

James Cock was born in Elgin, had very little education, and became a weaver at an early age. As a young man, he set off to emigrate to America, but the ship was driven ashore in Orkney, and he returned to Elgin to work at the weaver's trade. He started his married life at the age of twenty-three, he writes, with '2/6d capital'.

For some time, he was employed in Fraserburgh as a steward on the Saltoun estate, then returned to Elgin, where he struggled to make ends meet. He had, by this time, eight children. After a number of years, he moved to work in a linen factory at Grandholm Mills, Aberdeen, where, as far as we know, he lived until his death. He suffered ill-health for a considerable part of his life. Unable to work, for the purpose of making a little money, he published, in 1806, a book of verse entitled *Simple Strains: or homespun lays of an untutored muse*. He was the leader of a coterie of 'labouring poets' in the Woodside area of Aberdeen. Cock was always modest about his skills as *Epistle to Geordie* testifies. Two further editions, re-entitled *Hamespun Lays: or simple strains of an untutored muse*, were produced, in 1810 and 1820. In the introduction, he writes:

> 'Having, in youth, acquired the habit of early rising, it was my constant practice to repair to some of my

favourite retreats, of which, when at Elgin, I had three. One was, what is known by the name of the Bog of Oldmills; another, the Connet Hill, by the gentle stream of Lossie; a third was on the top of that hill above the church of New Spynie, whence stones are brought for building:

Hard by the margin of the waving wood,
In yonder grove, hard by the busy mill,
It fix'd my soul in awe and wonder, too.
Or on the banks of yonder winding rill,
Or on the summit of yon hill, I stood;
Such was the landscape open'd to my view.'

To a Mouse

Fu sall I tak my pen an write
Or tell you my unlucky fate?
The produce o my rhyming pate,
An some prose letters,
A mouse has torn them ilka bit
Just aa in tatters!

I've laboured twenty years an mair
The Muse's servant, late an ere
An clinket up poetic gear –
A thankless trade;
For gin we dinna mixt wi lear
We're ca'ed ill-bred.

To labour sic a length o time –
Compose, correct, an patch up rhyme
An try to gar my numbers chime
Wi easy twang,

James Cock (1752 – c.1824)

Ana to fill a creature's wame
Nae three inch lang.

Deil gi her neck were in a girn –
She's left me wi a raveled pirn;
Fu to behave, or whare to turn,
I dinna ken!
There's nae ae leaf but she has torn
Frae en to en.

Let ne'er my fae be in sic plight
As I was in that luckless night;
My rhymes in rags! A waefu sight,
Maist put me mad;
I fidged an flet an sobbed an sighed,
An ca'ed my head.

Had there been ony guid auld cheese
Or ony bits o candle grease
Or yet hard fish to chat an squeeze,
An stuff her kyte;
But tear my dry an sapless leaves
Was unco spite.

Cud she no ludged in barn or kil',
Or taen a beild at Habbie's mill,
An bored his saiks for corn or meal
An nae destroy't
The produce o the rhymin quill
    O simple poet?

To Nan (excerpt)
True love in sincerity form'd that cement
Which joined us together as one;
All the powers of black jealousy never could rent
Nor stain the sweet smiles of my Nan.

The hamlet was raise'd from the moss-covered sod,
Simplicity laid out the plan,
And rural felicity bless'd the abode
Which foster'd my lovely sweet Nan.

Thro forty long years of sweet wedlock we've gone,
Now wrinkles appear on our face;
With tender endearments thro life we go on,
With mutual contentment and peace.

Tho fled is the warmth of that mutual embrace,
Once glow'd in the bosom of youth;
Yet age, hoary age, loves the tender caress
Which flows from affection and truth.

Epistle to Geordie
Tho lang I've born the poet's name,
I hae sma right to public fame,
My muse at best's but unco lame,
Without a doubt;
But vain applause was not my aim
Fan I set out.

At first, she was fu stiff to draw,
For fup nor spur she wadna ca;
Necessity, that has nae law,
Gar't her tak gate;

James Cock (1752 – c.1824)

Tho mony a dowie day she saw,
She's aye on foot.
Guid scuds that fills a body's wame,
May whiles inspire a chiel to rhyme;
Vow Geordie, lad, ance on a time,
Fan just half fu,
I gart my numbers nicely chime
I sall avow.

Now, neiper, just to tell the truth,
My muse could frolic in her youth;
Fan she got aught to weet her mouth,
She rais'd a clatter—
Now fient a hait's to slok her drouth
But sups o water.

Robert Jamieson (1772 - 1844)

Robert Jamieson, was born on Spindlemuir, between Westfield and Roseisle, on 2 April 1772, the son of John Jamieson and Elizabeth Simpson. After attending Elgin Grammar School and graduating from King's College, Aberdeen, in 1793, he was appointed an assistant classical teacher at Macclesfield, Cheshire in 1796. Whilst there, he began to compile a collection of Scottish ballads and was engaged on this project for several years after 1800, in England, and while working as a tutor in Riga, in Latvia. He published, in 1806, two volumes entitled, *Popular ballads and songs, from tradition, manuscript, and scarce editions, with translations of similar pieces from the antient Danish language and a few originals by the editor.*

Sir Walter Scott held a high opinion of Jamieson, praising, in his *Border Minstrelsy,* Jamieson's discovery of the links between Scandinavian and Scottish ballads, ‹a circumstance which no antiquary had before so much as suspected›. A number of Jamieson's *Ballads* derive from manuscript transcripts made by Anna Gordon of Old Aberdeen (later known as Mrs Brown of Falkland) – a highly regarded source of traditional ballad variants.

In *Popular Ballads and Songs*, we find versions of *Sir Patrick Spence, Tifty's Annie, Lord Randall* and others. Like other song-collectors of the period, including Scott and Robert

Robert Jamieson (1772 – 1844)

Burns, Jamieson was presenting *his* version of the songs he found. He regularised the texts and sometimes proposed, or adapted, appropriate airs. He also composed his own songs, though, with considerable modesty, he admits that, 'on reading the productions of the Ayrshire Poet, I committed all, except two or three, to the flames'.

In his notes, Jamieson tells how *The Quern's Lilt* sprang from the following experience: as a youth he was travelling on foot between Fort Augustus and Inverness, when, nearly faint with hunger, he called at a cottage to beg for a little food. The woman spoke no English but took him in. She then 'went to the croft, cut down some barley; burnt the straw to dry the grain; and threw it up before the wind to separate it from the ashes; rubbed the grain between her hands, ground it upon a quern, sifted it, made a bannock of the meal and set it up to bake before the fire'. Within half-an-hour, he sat down, 'with wonder and delight', to a 'feast for a prince'.

Jamieson was a scholar of international reputation who made important contributions to the study of traditional ballads. In addition to his *Popular Ballads*, he edited, with Henry Weber and Sir Walter Scott, *Illustrations of Northern Antiquities* (1814); in 1818, he published a new edition of Edward Burt's *Letters from the North*.

For about thirty years, Jamieson, in part through Scott's influence, held a position in General Register House in Edinburgh, until about 1843.

For some reason he left that post to die a pauper in a Poorhouse in London, on 24 September, 1844.

My Wife's A Winsome Wee Thing.

My wife's a winsome wee thing,
A bonnie, blythesome wee thing,
My dear, my constant wee thing,

And evermair sall be;
It warms my heart to view her,
I canna choose but loe her,
And oh! weel may I trow her:
How dearly she loes me!

For though her face sae fair be,
As nane could ever mair be;
And though her wit sae rare be,
As seenil do we see;
Her beauty ne'er had gain'd me,
Her wit had ne'er enchain'd me,
Nor baith sae lang retain'd me
But for her love to me.

When wealth and pride disown'd me
Aa views were dark around me,
And sad and laigh she found me,
As friendless worth could be;
When ither hope gaed frae me
Her pity kind did stay me,
And love for love she gave me:
And that's the love for me!

And, till this heart is cald, I
That charm of life will hald by;
And, though my wife grow auld, my
Leal love aye young will be;
For she's my winsome wee thing,
My canty, blythesome wee thing,
My tender, constant wee thing,
And ever mair sall be.

Robert Jamieson (1772 – 1844)

The Quern's Lilt
The cronach stills the dowie heart
The jurram stills the bairnie;
The music for a hungry wame
Is grinding o the quernie.
And loes me o my little quernie!
Grind the gradden, grind it:
We'll aa get crowdie whan it's done,
And bannocks steeve to bind it.

The married man his joy may prize;
The lover prize his arles;
But gin the quernie gangna round,
They baith will soon be sareless.
Sae loes me, &c.

The whisky gars the bark o life
Drive merrily and rarely;
But graddan is the ballast gars
It steady gang and fairly.
Then loes me, &c.

Though winter steeks the door wi drift,
And oer the ingle hings us;
Let but the little quernie gae,
We're blythe, whatever dings us.
Then loes me, &c.

And how it cheers the herd at e'en,
And sets his heart-strings dirlin,
When, comin frae the hungry hill,
He hears the quernie birlin!
Then loes me, &c.

Though sturt and strife wi young and auld,
And flytin but and ben be;
Let but the quernie play, they'll soon
Aa lown and fidgin-fain be.
Then loes me o my little quernie!
Grind the gradden, grind it:
We'll aa get crowdie whan it's done,
And bannocks steeve to bind it.

John Grant (c. 1790 – c. 1840)

John Grant was born in Elgin in the later years of the eighteenth century. His widowed mother had very little means by which to provide anything other than the most elementary instruction for her five children. The elder two boys, James and John, were apprenticed to a baker. They spent all their spare time educating themselves and, in 1827, without a penny of capital, established the first newspaper in Moray, the *Elgin Courier*. The paper was not a success and closed down in 1834. James and John moved to London. James began a long and illustrious career in journalism, wrote forty books and published, in 1872, a three-volume history of the newspaper press. John set up as bookseller and publisher. John's first publication in London, in 1836, was his own composition, *The Penny Wedding*, the story of the meeting and marriage of Johnny Stewart and Jeanny Buie, from Pluscarden and Dallas, respectively. The project was inspired by Sir David Wilkie's painting of The Penny Wedding (1816). Grant writes:

'It was not an uncommon sight to witness from three to four hundred persons present at a penny wedding, enjoying themselves, alternately eating, drinking, and dancing; and as every man paid for what he eat and drank, besides contributing his share towards the remuneration of the fiddlers, and as the ceremonies connected with the wedding lasted four days, the profits on the articles supplied to such large concourses of people were a great acquisition to young couples, who married for love and had little to begin the world with, according to the estimation in which they were held by their friends and acquaintances.'

(*The Penny Wedding*, p2.)

The book has seven plates with lively drawings by Grant himself, illustrative of the progress of the marriage ceremony, from the Feet-Washing to the Bedding and Throwing the Stocking. There are also songs. The first printed here is sung by Jeanny's sister, Mary, to the best friend of the groom. The second song, sung by the bride's grandmother, introduces a chillier note.

John Grant died in London soon after the publication of *The Penny Wedding*.

Song 1
(Tune, 'Up and war them aa Willie'.)
O were ye e'er in love, laddie,
An met wi nae return;
Or were ye e'er in love, laddie,
An did yer bosom burn.

Wi striving to conceal the pain
That all true lovers feel,
When they hae little chance to gain
The ane they love so weel.

O were ye e'er in love, laddie,
An met wi cauld disdain;
From ane ye fondly doated on,

John Grant (c. 1790 – c. 1840)

An hop'd to caa yer ain.
If ye hae been in love, laddie,
An met a cauld return;
Ye'll ken what 'tis to love, laddie,
An hae yer bosom burn.

An may be ye may pity ane,
Who fondly doats on you;
An some day make her a yer ain,
For O, she loves ye true.

For I hae loved lang, laddie,
An I hae loved true;
But I hae never met, laddie,
Wi ony love frae you.

Song 2
(*Tune, 'The Land o the Leal'.*)
My bonny bairns sae blythe an gay
It pleases me tae see ye aa
Enjoy yerselves while yet ye may,
Before I'm taken far awa.
And Johnny, ye'll be kind to Jean
When she entrusts herself tae thee;
An make her happy when your ain,
In your sweet hame o Fallowlea.

My age is now fourscore an nine,
My time on earth can but be sma;
But I am pleased that she'll be thine,
Before I'm taken far awa.
But O, it grieves me sair to see
The change that's comin o'er ye aa,

By following customs strange to me,
That hae been brocht frae far awa.

When I was bonny blythe an young,
A happy time that was tae me!
I then could dance and sing a song,
While herding on the summer lea.

An I hae joined the merry throng
O lads an lasses full o glee:
In winter when the nichts were lang,
To meet the lad was dear tae me.

An I hae danced the highland reel,
At rants an tweddles, wi great glee,
Wi the dear lad I loed sae weel,
An none did ere find faut wi me.

But noo the times are altered sair,
There's little pastime tae be seen,
When we go tae the country fair,
Or to the market on the green.

The tweddles an the pleasant rant,
Sae common as they used tae be,
Are changed for politics an cant
An fondness for the barley-bree.

John Milne of Glenlivat (sic) (1792 – 1871)

'While his rugged numbers and unceremonious sarcasms gave immense satisfaction to his patrons of the farm-servant class, and drew many a copper from their pockets, he took a general interest in all subjects, political, religious, and social. Left to his own impulses, his sympathies were always with the suffering and the struggling, with honest poverty and true merit. And, in short, if there was a grievance to redress – national, local or personal – his pen was always ready.'

The Songs and Poems (1871) p xiv

The anonymous author of the introduction to John Milne's *Songs and Poems* (1871) presents Milne as the archetypal itinerant poet of the first half of the nineteenth century. He recalls:

'seeing *[Milne]* riding leisurely along the Inverness turnpike on his favourite ass – which was his faithful servant for twenty years – with his plaid about his shoulders, "his guid blue bonnet" upon his head, and his wallet replenished with newly printed ballads slung by his side. Doubtless he was fresh from the printer, *en route* for

Glenlivat, furnished for the coming term's feeing markets with songs and poems, new as well as old'.

Orphaned by the age of five, brought up, along with his four brothers, by his paternal grandfather at Netherley, Kincardineshire, Milne received one month of education in three successive winters, was apprenticed as a shoemaker, moved to Demick, a remote croft on the Braes of Glenlivet, began whisky-smuggling, suffered from recurring ill-health, and took up writing verse. For over thirty years, his life was:

> 'spent going hither and thither in pursuit of his vocation. Those who have seen him as he stood surrounded by a group of noisily appreciative rustics, stick in hand, with the invariable knee breeches, tartan plaid and blue bonnet, delivering the last "New Song" in his own peculiar chant, with abundant facial expression, and quaint emphasis will not readily forget the scene'.

Milne was clearly as much a performer as poet and he sold his poems on broadsheets in numbers to 'appreciative rustics', across the North and as far South as Edinburgh. He was a Radical, profoundly anti-Tory, the only one of the poets in this collection who was openly political. He wrote on the Repeal of the Corn Laws, the Disruption of the Church of Scotland, the evils of Catholicism, the ill-treatment of British troops (by the politicians who had sent them there) during the Crimean War, and on the participants in local elections:

> 'Better be back among his slaves
> Than be the Tory Jack of Knaves,
> Brave Duff defeated Arndilly
> That Tory laird, sunburnt and silly.'

John Milne of Glenlivat (sic) (1792 – 1871)

Another writer, Alexander Mitchell, in his *Recollections* (1911), tells us that, 'if there was a disagreement at any farm, the farm servants would send the details to Johnnie Milne, and he would then compose his verses and sell them at the feeing market'.

And so, we see that the poet performed a certain 'political' function in the on-going struggle between masters and men.

John Milne died at Cullerlie on lower Deeside, after a long illness, having seen his wife and six of his ten children die before him.

The Reformer's Song

Ye lads an bonny lasses aa,
Whate'er's yer occupation,
There's naething new frae wig tae wa
But light an reformation.

Our nation's back is like tae brak
Wi taxes an wi pensions,
I'm feared she's gaun tae jail for debt,
Tae glimmer through the stanchions.

For honest men tae mak the laws,
Ye aa should vote by ballot.
I think it's best tae write yer names
An stap them in a wallet.

For fouk can only please themsels,
An let naebody thraw them,
I think it's aye the fairest way,
Like Valentine tae draw them.
Or bring me forth an honest man,
Devoid of selfish nonsense,

I winna care what wey they vote,
But dae it for yer conscience.

When honesty lifts up her heid,
She's chokit wi the warl,
For ye man hae a sappy slice,
An I maun hae a farl.

I neither would hae dukes nor lords
For tae get yearly pensions,
It would be best bestowed on those
That make the steam inventions.

The ships and coaches run by steam,
Steam ploos they are preparing
An some do say, that yet by steam,
Well flee fae here tae Erin.

Lands, dukes, and lords great rents afford,
Which might support them fairly,
All may agree and plainly see,
That they are pensioned yearly.

Millions of sinecures they give
Tae nobles for assistance,
Such as a Master o the Hawks
An posts nae in existence.

I now do hope the days are come
Tae renovate our nation,
An downright honesty itsel's
The road tae exaltation.
We'll maybe get a cog o ale

John Milne of Glenlivat (sic) (1792 – 1871)

Tae clear oor wizened paunches,
A buttered bannock tae oor mous
An breeks tae hap oor haunches.

Perfection disna come at ance
Tae man nor yet tae nation.
It took a while tae raise the pile
An finish the Creation.

But perseverance winna ding
When ance it taks the notion.
It turns the mountains heels ower heid
An elevates the ocean.

Success tae every honest man
May truth direct him fairly;
A happy lifetime tae oor Queen,
I wish her weel sincerely.

A merry weddin, soon an sure
Tae every pretty maiden;
A girnal cramm'd wi meal an flour
An purses heavy laden.

William Hay (1794 - 1854)

In his '*Recollections*', published in the *Elgin and Morayshire Courier*, in 1855, William Rhind wrote:

> 'William Hay was born in Elgin about the year 1794, in a tenement in the White Horse Close. His father he never saw nor knew. Under his mother's care he passed his infant and boyish years, sharing such treatment as her precarious means – the retail of small wares from a stall in the market – and perhaps somewhat improvident mode of life afforded'.

As a street urchin, 'half-clothed and half-fed', Hay must have 'possessed superior attractions' for he very early attracted a number of generous friends and patrons. One was Mrs Innes of the White Horse Inn, in Elgin, another was Mr Anderson, classical teacher at the newly established Elgin Academy, where the boy was to receive full education free of charge. He was a model student and was 'dux' of every class he attended. Lack of money ruled out attendance at university, and, in 1814, he began – with the family of Cumming, at Logie on the Findhorn – a career of private tutoring which was to last throughout his working life. In 1818, the Cumming family moved to Edinburgh and Hay moved with them. He loved

William Hay (1794 – 1854)

Edinburgh – the life of the place and the opportunities it offered. His plan was to maintain himself as a 'flying' tutor, and, at the same time to attend the University classes he needed to fit him for the church. For about twenty-five years, he led a busy, active, and sociable life among the academics and the literati of the day – in particular, the influential circle around William Blackwood's *Edinburgh Magazine*. Apparently, he seldom returned to Moray but always sent money to maintain his ageing mother.

In 1824, the Edinburgh Morayshire Club was formed by 'exiles.' Hay was appointed their poet laureate, producing songs and poems, celebrating the homeland. These were performed at the Club's meetings, and, in 1851, a collection was published by the *Forres Gazette*, under the title *The Lintie o Moray*. In the 1830s and 1840s, Hay's translations of classical Greek and Latin verse were published regularly in *Blackwood's Magazine* and came under sharp scrutiny; however, it is for the poems in *The Lintie* that Hay is best remembered.

For the last ten years of his life, Will Hay was afflicted by what we would probably call depression, then by blindness, and finally by paralysis of his lower limbs. He stayed in the home of friends, never leaving the house. He was buried in the New Calton Cemetery.

The Bonnie Land o Moray
(Tune – 'Woo'd an married an aa'.)
Come join me, my Morayshireeners,
Wi each a glass in his hand,
In a hearty good bumper and chorus,
To the weal o our ain fatherland,
Where the Findhorn, the Spey, and the Lossie,
Frae the mountains roll down to the main,

Poetry of Moray

And gladden the meadows and valleys
Sae fertile in fruit and in grain.
Elgin and Forres an aa,
Forres and Elgin an aa;
And are na loons very weel aff,
That were born in ane o the twa?

'Tis the land where those jolly old fellows,
The Monks, once revelled at feasts,
In their kirks, and cathedrals, and abbeys
And are we not the sons o the priests?
Yes! our fathers were rough, fighting billies,
And slashed ane anither like beasts;
While our mothers, the pious, good women,
Were praying alang wi the priests.
Elgin and Forres, &c.

Oh, Elgin! Thou glory o Moray!
The priest, the cross, and the dirk
Are gane wi their fastings and fightings,
And still thou'rt the friend o the kirk.
Thou hast kirks for all sects and Seceders,
Where no flaws o heresy lurk;
And he's but a heretic sinner,
That wishes not weel to the kirk.
Elgin and Forres, &c.

'Tis the land where the lasses are lovely,
And loving as much as you please,
Where their feeties instead o their fingers,
They use when bleaching their claes.
'Tis the land where George Edward, the drummer,
The most thrifty and waukrife o men,

William Hay (1794 – 1854)

Wi his row-row-de-dow in the morning,
Awakes you – to slumber again.
Elgin and Forres, &c.

'Tis the land where cheap is our living,
And cheaper our learning at schools;
'Tis the land abounding in wisdom,
And superabounding in fools.
'Tis the land abounding in daft folks,
And these are our glory and pride,
Since genius, the poet hath told us,
To madness is ever allied.
Elgin and Forres, &c.

'Tis the land o Tam Spiers, and o 'Scravie'
Who o liars was surely the chief.
'Tis the land o the 'Garb' and Tam Watson,
The land o 'Blin Jamie' the thief.
'Tis the land o 'Mad Chalmers,' whose 'buckies'
Were curiously fixed on his hair;
'Mad Innes,' 'Mad Russell', 'Feel Robbie',
'Feel Clarkie,' the snuffer – are there.
Elgin and Forres, &c.

'Tis the land o the famed Knock o Alves,
Where fairies and spirits repair,
To revel and dance on the moonbeams,
Or trip it o'er meadows o air.
'Tis the land where witches and warlocks,
Wi Satan hae played mony pranks;
'Tis the land o the Elgin Cathedral,
And the 'Bishop o Moray' – John Shanks.
Elgin and Forres, &c.

When This Auld Coat Was New
(Tune – 'Hey! Quo Bob and John.')

When this auld coat was new,
Sin syne 'tis thirty years, Sir!
Auld Elgin toon excelled
Ilk toon baith far an near, Sir!
A monkish lookin toon,
Most reverend for to view, Sir!
O! `tis altered for the worse,
Since this auld coat was new, Sir!
Elgin was a toon,
A toon to live an dee in;
But noo it is a hole,
Which few would care to be in.

Ilk house was thatched wi strae,
Or slate o sober grey, Sir!
Where martin-swallows found
A shelter nicht an day, Sir!
Wi just a single street,
Though backsides it had two, Sir!
What a goodly town it was
When this auld coat was new, Sir!
Elgin was a toon, &c.

Its biggins a'maist aa
Turned their gables to the street, Sir!
Its causeway had a 'croon,'
For proud an haughty feet, Sir!
Piazzas it had some,
An bow yetts not a few, Sir!
An a lion crested cross,

William Hay (1794 – 1854)

When this auld coat was new, Sir!
Elgin was a toon, &c.

An Thunderton upreared
Its bartizan sae crouse, Sir!
An wailing ghosts were heard
In Dr Dougal's house, Sir!
Where deeds without a name,
That made one's spirit grue, Sir!
Were done; but aa is gane,
Since this auld coat was new, Sir!
Elgin was a toon, &c.

An then the Muckle Kirk,
That gem on Elgin's brow, Sir!
O cunning mason-work;
Alas! Where is it now, Sir?
My ban upon ye aa,
Ye senseless, tasteless crew, Sirs!
What have ye got instead,
Since this auld coat was new, Sir!
Elgin was a toon, &c.

Ay! Licht yer kirk wi' gas,
Ye non-obtrusion sumphs, Sirs!
Silk purse ye canna mak
O lug o sow that grumphs, Sirs!
But where the thousand lichts
Which a blaze o splendour threw, Sir!
Oer the auld kirk's pillared aisles,
When this auld coat was new, Sir?
Elgin was a toon, &c.

Poetry of Moray

At the great and solemn feast,
When the chandeliers were lit, Sir!
And visions, not of earth,
Athwart our minds did flit, Sir!
O! the true in life is false,
The false alone is true, Sir!
Then gie us back the past,
When this auld coat was new, Sir!
Elgin was a toon, &c.

The Chanry's ivied walls,
Wi fog o time all hoar, Sir!
Where pilgrims came to weep,
To worship and adore, Sir!
The sanctities o time,
Their mantle oer her threw, Sir!
When this auld coat was new, Sir!
Elgin was a toon, &c.

Even her, some Elgin Goth
Most impiously did wish, Sir!
To improve into a shed,
For fish-wives to sell their fish, Sir!
He moans their mogganed legs,
Frost bitten black and blue, Sir!
They hadna legs ava,
When this auld coat was new, Sir!
Elgin was a toon, &c.

My bonnie Ladyhill,
Fu vauntie be thy looks, Ma'am!
Thy name is linked wi his,
The last o Moray's dukes, Ma'am!

William Hay (1794 – 1854)

Green was thy gowaned sward,
Where paper-dragons flew, Ma'am!
And litted eggs were row'd,
When this auld coat was new, Ma'am!
Elgin was a toon, &c.

Wild were the Lossie's banks,
An free the Gallows Green, Sir!
Where many a game at 'chow'
In former days was seen, Sir!
Tam Spiers, my brither, - Tam,
What are they noo, - say you Sir?
'Trim as my Nanny's mutch!'
Since this auld coat was new, Sir!
Elgin was a toon, &c.

The Shambles, too, must feel
Reform's relentless sheers, Sir!
That storehouse o the stink
O some twa hunder years, Sir!
In your Museum, place
That smell, that folks may view, Sirs!
What Elgin noses were,
When this auld coat was new, Sirs!
Elgin was a toon, &c.

That antiquated thing,
The Jail, is going too, Sir!
It seems it canna haud
The rogues that flourish noo, Sir!
'Twas empty in the days
O honest men and true, Sir!
But Elgin's much reformed

Since this auld coat was new, Sir!
Elgin was a toon, &c.

Now, Shirra Innes, Sir!
(There's Moray blood in thee, Sir!)
If you're a Jail Commissioner,
(And such I trow you be, Sir!)
Step forth and save that Jail,
That future times may view, Sir!
What Elgin biggins were,
When this auld coat was new, Sirs!
Elgin was a toon, &c.

Sir Robert o Gordonstoun

O! Wha has na heard o that man o renown –
The wizard, Sir Robert o Gordonstoun?
The wisest o warlocks – the Morayshire chiel, –
The despot o Duffus, an frien o the Deil!
The man whom the folks o auld Morayshire feared –
The man whom the fiends o auld Satan revered, –
O! never to mortal was evil renown
Like that o Sir Robert o Gordonstoun! –
What a wicked auld loon
Was this Morayshire loon!

The sun he might in the east or the wast,
But Sir Robert's wee body nae shadow could cast;
Langsyne had he lost it in far foreign parts,
When he cheated the Deil in the school o Black Arts.
'The *hurly-buck-out* o the school is *my* fee,'
Cried Satan – 'an surely Sir Robert is he.'
'Look behin,' cried Sir Robert, 'there tak him, thou loon!'

William Hay (1794 – 1854)

Twas the shadow o Robert o Gordonstoun!
What a crafty auld loon
Was this Morayshire loon!

How fiercely the furnace at Gordonstoun glows! –
At Gordonstoun, famous for witches an crows!
Seven years hath Sir Robert been toilin wi micht,
Till a fiend-salamander hath gladdened his sicht!
'Hurra!' cried Sir Robert, an the creature cried 'Here!
Ye witches an warlocks o Moray draw near!' –
An loud is the din o the demons that own
Their master, Sir Robert o Gordonstoun!
What a terrible loon
Was this Morayshire loon!

Far up in the lift are the sternies o nicht,
Oer the ice-sheeted Spynie loch blinkin sae bricht;
But so tender that ice, that it maunna be press'd,
For it yields to the wecht o the waterfowl's breast.
But what cares Sir Robert for the ice or the hour!
He's out on the loch in his chariot an four;
An it cracks, an it rattles, but daurna gang down –
Sic power hath Sir Robert o Gordonstoun!
What a venturesome loon
Was this Morayshire loon!

Sawney Phulp! Sawney Phulp! thou coachman sae bold,
Thou art het eneuch here, though the nicht it be cold;
An the sweat frae thy ee-brow is tricklin in beads; –
But lookna behin – or thou'rt meat for the geds!
For a legion o witches are close in thy wake,
An a corbie's behin wi the ee o a snake;
But wha is that corbie, wi Beelzie's ain frown?

O! that awfu'some loon –
O! that Morayshire loon!

Twa cronies, at midnicht, in Gordonstoun Haa,
Are boozin – an mony's the bicker they draw;
They drew an they drank, an were ne'er like to tire, –
For it fizz'd frae their stamacks like water frae fire!
That frien o Sir Robert's is Reverend to see
As the Parson o Duffus – but it canna be he –
For a chaulder o maut the drouth didna droon,
O that guest o Sir Robert o Gordonstoun!
O! the drouth o the loon –
What a boozin auld loon!

Sir Robert could drink like a Morayshire chiel –
But a man has sma chance that would drink wi the Deil;
Sir Robert got fuddled; – when upstarted his guest
On all fours – an nicker'd in shape o a beast.
'Gee up!' cried Sir Robert, an sprang on the back
O that fierce-lookin charger, so fiery an black;
An, bang through the window, for Birnie are boun'
The Deil an Sir Robert o Gordonstoun!
Losh! sic a queer loon
Was this Morayshire loon!

Like the blast o the North was the speed o their flicht,
As they thunder'd alang through the mirk o the nicht;
They dash'd thro Loch Spynie, near Duffus strong keep,
An Findrassie's echoes aroused from their sleep; –
They leap'd oer the Lossie, – an Elgin's lang street
Flashed fire, an re-echoed the trampin o feet; –
An the burghers cried, 'Save us! that's surely Mahoun,
Or that fearfu Sir Robert o Gordonstoun!

William Hay (1794 – 1854)

Preserve's frae that loon –
O! that awfu some loon!'
Sir Robert leugh sair, – an his horse leugh too,
When Birnie's green hillocks now gladden'd their view;
For loud was the cheerin that greeted them there,
Frae the sprites o the earth, an fiends o the air.
There the witches o Moray were dancin wi' glee,
'Mid music an mirth, an loud revelrie;
For the Parson o Birnie has put himsel doon.
Preserve's frae Sir Robert o Gordonstoun!
O! that waefu'some loon!
O! that Morayshire loon!

(According to the New Statistical Account of Scotland *(1845), the subject of Hay's poem, Sir Robert Gordon, 3rd Baronet,*

> *'made himself master of many secrets in natural history unknown to his illiterate countrymen, whom he took pleasure in frightening and astonishing. It was believed that he was educated in Italy in the School of the Black Art'.*

Legends abounded. He had some commitment to science and engineering. He invented a water pump that was tested by the Navy and he was elected to the Royal Society in 1686.)

James Murdoch – 'Cutler Jamie'
(1806 – 1872)

'Cutler Jamie' is an example of the self-taught, itinerant writer of verse. In 1863, he published a collection of the pieces that had appeared over the years in the *Elgin Courant*. The collection includes an autobiographical sketch, which, to be frank, may be of more interest to the modern reader than the poems that follow it. The Preface sets the tone:

> 'If this publication prove anything like remunerative, I will feel grateful; but if it shall do otherwise, it will only add one more to the many schemes that have proved abortive in the hands of the writer.'

Born in Mosstowie, James Murdoch was brought up 'in abject poverty and taught to look forward to a life of rustic serfdom'. He started work as a cattle herder at the age of twelve; however, 'from the earliest period, [his] mind was naturally thoughtful, keenly sensitive, and strongly inclined to sensual enjoyment'. He 'acquired a set of foppish notions' and came to hate his employers for treating him as an inferior. At fifteen, he managed to put himself 'a few months to school' on a crash course of English grammar, Arithmetic and Latin. He took a job as a packman, buying and selling second-hand items,

James Murdoch – 'Cutler Jamie' (1806 – 1872)

including books, around the doors of the country, from John o' Groats to Dover in Kent. He admits that 'this was the happiest and most prosperous period that I can remember of my life'. However, on returning to Elgin, he 'fell into dissolute and dissipated company' that led to 'states of inebriety for weeks together' and nearly to his death.

Shocked into sobriety, he went back to farm work but he despised his 'companions of labour' – 'their extreme willful ignorance, the contempt in which they held everything that exercises the mind'. He returned to life on the road as a packman and, by chance, fell into training as a knife-grinder in Sheffield, where he stayed for some years before returning to Elgin to work as an itinerant knife-grinder with his own grinding-wheel on a 'hurley', sharpening and repairing cutlery. Hence, his nom de plume.

A year or so later, he married 'an Edinburgh girl'. They took to the road and followed a wandering life for four years before returning to a 'little cot' at Whitefield, Mosstowie, and to the knife-grinding. His wife earned the 'most part of her own living by doing field-work with neighbouring farmers' until she was disabled 'by a violent attack of scrofula'. For the rest of their lives, they remained on the Poor Register, close to destitution. Jamie died in 1871, his wife three years later.

Cutler Jamie was another poet of the *Elgin Courant*. His poems appeared week after week over a number of years. They are, almost exclusively, profoundly gloomy. Subjects include infanticide, suicide, poverty, drunkenness, slavery, delusions, and brutish sex. Language and poetic forms range from the high-flown to the banal and almost meaningless. He did not use Scots.

The poem that follows tells a local story: the Kirk Sink is a small hollow, near Cutler Jamie's home which was at the south-east corner of Heldon Hill. Legend had it that on one

Sunday morning, the church, full to capacity, fell into a sinkhole.

The Doom of The Kirk
There stood the church, on that green spot,
Now covr'd with the sod
The house in which the people met
To offer praise to God.
For many a day the voice of prayer
Was heard within its walls;
But on one day its fate was sealed,
As oft an empire falls.

Upon a pleasant Sabbath morn,
All nature dressed in smiles,
The people crowded to that church
From many distant miles.
The morning bell had also sent
Its summons through the air;
The pious loved to hear the sound
That summoned them to prayer.

Now all around the church is filled
With people crowded in;
The parson's risen to his feet,
The service to begin.
The book's turned o'er, the Psalm is read,
The song of praise is sung.
And the parson's voice ascends in prayer
For all, both old and young.

When suddenly a crash was heard
The earth gave way below,

James Murdoch – 'Cutler Jamie' (1806 – 1872)

And down, and down, the Gothic walls
And vaulted roof did go.
I think I hear that horrid cry,
That soon was hushed in death,
And never more was heard again
From them who sank beneath.

I think I see the people round
Assembled at the place,
Lamenting their departed friends
With many a tearful face.
A helpless infant's lost its nurse,
A mother's lost her son,
A lover's lost his heart's delight,
His love is sunk within.

And never more the light of heaven
Shall pierce the dismal gloom
That reigns within these sunken walls
Which thus became their tomb.
And never shall a sound be heard
Within these walls again,
Till the last trumpet's awful blast
A hearing shall obtain.

Then darksome is yon thunder cloud,
Approaching on the wind,
But darker must have been the hopes
Of them thus left behind;
And darker still the dismal gloom
That reigns among the dead,
Entombed beneath that sunken roof
Till their last doom be read.

William Hay Leith Tester – 'La Teste' (1829 – 1892)

In the eighth 'Edition' of his poems (1886), La Teste published the following *Criticism Sketch by Mr AG Murdoch, of Glasgow*:

'William HL Tester – better known by his nom de plume La Teste – was born on the royal domain of Balmoral, parish of Crathie, Aberdeenshire, February 28, 1829. He received a good ordinary education and, in his thirteenth year, began the business of life as a page to the late Lady Abergeldie, then resident at Westerton House, romantically situated in the secluded valley of Pluscarden, six miles distant from Elgin. In this vocation – as footman, valet and butler – he had opportunities of seeing a good deal of life, both at home and abroad, which has been turned to good account in several of his poems. La Teste early discovered a fertile faculty for versatile verse-writing. His books make capital reading. His fancy is bright and pleasing, his diction choice, his flow spontaneous and musical, and his native enthusiasm unbounded …

La Teste's writings, like the verses of all poets in humble life, are unequal in interest and merit. He has great

William Hay Leith Tester – 'La Teste' (1829 – 1892)

facility of composition, however, and if he has written much, he has also, it must be conceded, written well. His career has, from the first, been a varied and somewhat chequered one, and for years he has struggled through poverty and despair in the ceaseless exercise of his legitimate function of verse-making. He is now almost totally deprived of vision. He is *par excellence* the poet of the *Elgin Courant*, to the 'Poet's Corner' of which north country journal, he has popularly contributed for the greater part of a quarter of a century.'

It is clear that 'La Teste' wasted nearly every penny that he ever made, mostly through drink. He and his family – he married twice – occupied a room in the most degraded of all High Street closes, known as Little Hell. On one occasion, he composed an epitaph to be used in the event of his wife's death:

Here lies Bell Clark in her clean linen sark,
Wha in life, Sir, 'twas thocht was a trig ane;
But noo in her pride, she has flown from my side
And left Little Hell for the Big ane.

Many of his poems glorify the wonders of whisky; a few depict, movingly, the effects of excessive drinking. By his early forties, he had become an inmate, for the first time, of the Morayshire Union Poorhouse in Bishopmill – Peter's Palace. By his mid-fifties he was nearly blind. Further admissions to what became 'Craigmoray' followed until he died there after a period of severe illness in 1892. His tenth 'Edition' – what La Teste referred to as 'Editions' were completely new collections, with some old favourites thrown in – was published in 1890. As 'Poet Laureate of Lodge Kilmolymock', he was buried at the Cathedral with full Masonic honours.

Peter's Palace
Peter Grant was the first Governor, or Warden, of the new Morayshire Union Poorhouse, later named Craigmoray, in Bishopmill.

Peter, get yer Palace ready,
Tak us wi ye, ane an aa;
Gude preserve us, sic a Friday –
Saw ye ever sic a snaw?

The like was never seen in Moray;
Keenly felt puir labourin folks –
Nocht in the hoose but want an sorrow,
Rumblin wymes an toom meal pyocks …

I canna write nae mair – I'm greetin –
Ilka cloud as black as death;
The twa bit bairns like lammies bleatin,
For they're caul and hungry baith!

Peter get yer Palace ready –
Tak us aa tae Bishopmill –
We're hungry, haggard, nakit, needy!
Be thou our good St Peter still.

The Sunday Mornin Woman

Tak tent hoo she teets roun the mou o the close,
Did ever ye see sic a sicht – sic a soce?
Her phiz looks as if – it's sae clootit and scrattit,
It ne'er had been soosht sin the howdie was at it.

She's a rare lookin pattern o she-manifactur,
An seems as if hir'd by some tattie contractur

William Hay Leith Tester – 'La Teste' (1829 – 1892)

To fleg awa vermin, whan plantin the same,
Bein a bundle o rags ower a skeleton frame.

Her mutch, whilk hauf-hidit her wiry grey hair,
Was sombre aneuch, an the waur o the wear!
Her vrapper an coattie wadna fetch'd hauf a groat,
Ae houch had a stockin, but the ither had not.

In her left breest the 'cutter' was carefully stow'd,
Lack-a-day, she wad gi'en a deid Peabody's gowd
To get it replenished wi a saxpenny gill,
For she shook in ilk nerve, an look'd yawfully ill.

She had bocht a 'hauf-peck,' an took in yesternicht,
As thirsty folk should, whether wrongous or richt,
Tho she ca'd ilka neuk in the hole – och! hon!
Deil a skyte cud be gotten – for the nectar was gone!

Assur'd the 'blue beetle' was aff o his beat,
Some courage she muster'd, an tript up the street,
In the hope o procurin, like mair folk, a bead,
O which she stood sairly this mornin in need.

The wealthy can slip to the sideboard an tak
Their brandy an soda, rare sherry an sack;
But this poortith-struck sister, sae wizen'd an wan,
Maun raise a 'refresher' the best wey she can.

She tried aa the publics, but nocht like success
Her efforts wad croon, tho chin-deep in distress,
Sae raggit in garment, wi bruik sae besmeart,
The gin-vendor Christians were fleggit to gie'rt.

She steered her frail yacht towards mysel ower the street,
She noddit, peer body, an was maist like to greet,
And in accents o woe, which I cudna weel thole,
Quo she – 'Willie, man, wad ye succour a soul?'

She was aince a gran templar, an fusky-folk 'smashed'.
But return'd to the mire, like the soo that was wash'd,
An her reason, peer craytur, some wey or anither,
Like Rob's 'Tam o Shanter,' got tint aathegither.

Tis an awfu thing 'Drooth'. Whan yer throat's in a hell,
(I've sometimes been fash'd wi a furnace mysel'),
Sae I pitied her case in my ain little mind
Fellow-feelins, ye ken, mak us wonderfu kind.

I kent o a hovel, they ca a 'shebeen,'
I got her the 'needfu' – may I be forgi'en.
I did it for gweed – tho I often hae said,
We sudna encourage illegitimate trade.

I gaed her a yaird o advice, to be sure;
To abstain was her only effectual cure,
An three times on Sunday to start for the kirk,
Wi' a face on as lang as the tail o a stirk.

An mind whan ye swallow a 'nip' on the sly,
As the maist o saunts do, whilk they canna deny,
Chew a moufu o garlic, an then, by my faith,
They'll be bold wha wad dare tak a smell o yer breath.

My Wee Cripple Wean

Her leggie was broken whan her mither lay dyin,
An death took oor new-born bairnie awa;

William Hay Leith Tester – 'La Teste' (1829 – 1892)

There was naething but poortith, an sabbin an sighin,
For it seem'd as if Heaven had forsaken us aa
Ere her soul sunward soar'd, that a towmond had flutter'd
For freedom, to bask in Omnipotence' sheen;
My heart maistly rent when her last words were utter'd:
'Willie, be good to oor wee cripple wean.'

Years hae roll'd on sin the sod happ'd her mither;
Whiles we've been dowie, an whiles we've been glad,
An whiles whan we're cantie an coortin thegither,
A stranger micht tak's for a lass an a lad.
In the weird wintry time, whan lang wark made me weary,
Frae chanticleer's matin to vesper at e'en,
The click o her staff on the stanes made me cheery,
Whan, smiling, she met me – my wee cripple wean.

Twas a cauld cabin oors, for twas rottin an fa'in;
Sometimes we had fire, an sometimes we had nane;
An we cudna help shiverin when Boreas was blawin
The 'beautiful snow' thro the auld crackit pane.
Tho oor bits o bed trappin were no unco cosey,
We cuddled the closer an steekit oor een,
An I felt mair than happy whan, sleepin sae rosy,
She dream'd in my oxter – my wee cripple wean.

She grew grave at her pray'rs, an she learn'd her carritch,
An sang hymns o heaven wi an organ-like swell;
An at nicht, whan the dear thing had suppit her parritch,
I wash'd wi a will her bit duddies mysel.
Oor gear bein scant, unbefriended, unaided,
I mendit her stockins an clootit her sheen;

An blithe beat my breast as the broon curls I braided
That kiss'd the broad broo o my wee cripple wean.

She's a little Minerva in wisdom, the kitty –
Ye'd wonder hoo words come sae glib to her tongue;
Her funny remarkin, sae wise-like an witty,
Amuses the auld an dumbfoonders the young.
A Venus in beauty, as modest's a gowan,
A seraph in mind, a Madonna in mien,
Wi a heartie sae tender, sae lovin, sae lowin,
She's aa body's body – my wee cripple wean.

The clouds that sae lang hae been hovering oer us,
Hope's balmiest breezes are driving away;
An I'll live yet to sing ye a cheerier chorus
While Tibbuck's the love an the licht o my lay.
I dootna some day she'll astonish the warl,
An the warl mayhap hail her Poetry's Queen,
Wi a haa o her ain, an a garland o laurel
Be wreath'd roond the broo o my wee cripple wean.

An A.B.C of Notable Places.
Aberdeen, auld Scotlan's Granite City,
Lang famous for Devanha's aque veetie.

Banff, whaur blithe M'Pherson in his glee
The fiddle played 'Anaith the gallows tree.'

Cockpen, the laird o the Whilk wha wed,
Not the braw lady, but the lady's maid.

Devil's Den, an dismal dens they are,
The mair we preach against, they grow the waur.

William Hay Leith Tester – 'La Teste' (1829 – 1892)

Elgin, whilk a parson ca'd in sorrow,
Hoo horrible! A – 'Sodom an Gomorrah.'

Falkirk, whilk you've read sae much about,
Whaur Hielan drovers gang to sell their nowte.

Grantown, gin yer fond o scenery wild,
Gang there in simmer, whan the season's mild.

Helmsdale, the coast for ling and cod,
An herrin, whyles, for half-a-croon the load.

Inverness, whaur Bessie Wat can melt
Their whinstane hairts, as soon's her song is felt.

John o Groats, a rare auld Caithness carl,
Wha made some sough, like mair folk, in the warl.

Killie, sung by Rab, the rantin boy,
For nicht-keps famous – black an red Rob Roy.

Letterfourie, whaur Sir Robert lives,
A kindly knicht, wha never taks, but gives.

Mark'd Minmore, in Livet's lovely glen,
Whaur Major Smith is reckon'd – King o Men.

Nairn, gin ye gang there to bathe an bide,
The Cally Host will prove yer freend an guide.

Old Meldrum, gin yer fond o snuff,
Ye'll get it there delicious, sure enuff.

Poetry of Moray

Paisley, famous in the weavin art,
Whaur Tannahill's sweet muse was drooned in Carte.

Queensferry, whaur the railway brig
Will soon be ope'd to hurl ower peer an pig.

Randolph's spacious Hall, in whilk micht stan
Cornel M'Kenzie's 'thousand-braves-an-one'.

Stromness, on fair Pomona's shore,
Round which the angry billows roll an roar.

Tomintoul, the chief o aa retreats
To those wha love sweet solitude an peats.

Ulvah's Isle, by Hielan Caumel sung,
In whilk a race o reivin rogues up-sprung.

Vale o Auford, that's the simmer spot
For Aberdonians, holidays or not.

Wick, the light thereof, King Grant,
As lang's his Ensign's hale an good his plant.

Xeter, a howf in whilk Salvation
Battalions rave – that reef-raff o the nation.

Yang-t-Yang-Sing-Sunk-t-Kung-King-eena,
Ye'll find it somewhere in the map o Cheena.

Zanzibar, whaur Livingstone, some think,
Kept a slave-market inn, an selt Scotch drink.

Frank Sutherland – 'Uncle Peter'
(1837–1920)

On 17 December, 1878, at the Annual Festival of the London Morayshire Club, the winner of a competition for a club song, to be entitled *Morayland*, was announced, and the song sung for the first time. Thirty-one songs had been submitted. The winner was Frank Sutherland ('Uncle Peter'), Elgin. His prize was three guineas, 'an amount generously supplemented to five guineas, by Mr A Simpson'. The song begins,

> 'Ance mair aroon this festive board
> Convenes oor social band –
> A lot o leal an loyal loons
> Frae dear aul Morayland'

and rattles on as follows for a dozen stanzas,

> 'Though far-removed, we still can see
> Yon shady Oakwood dell,
> The auld Bow Brig, green Lady Hill
> And trickling Marywell.'

Born in Elgin, Frank Sutherland made his living as a barber, working in Elgin and Forres. He was a skilled musician; he and his two brothers forming 'Sutherland's Orchestra'. They featured regularly at dances in the Assembly Rooms in Elgin and played before royalty at Dunrobin Castle. The family was very much part of the northern musical community. Frank Sutherland's son married the daughter of J Scott Skinner, 'The Strathspey King', who lived in Elgin for a number of years.

'Uncle Peter's' collection of poems, *Sunny Memories of Morayland*, was published in 1883. The title carries an interesting echo of Mrs Harriet Beecher Stowe's *Sunny Memories of Many Lands* (1854). Perhaps, he is saying that we don't need to travel all over the world to generate 'sunny memories.'

Over many years, Sutherland contributed pieces to the *Northern Scot* and the *Courant*. His poems, often in Scots, focus largely on the life and characters of lowland Moray. 'Poetic merit,' he says, 'I do not think they possess'. His intention, he says, has always been to amuse. In one poem he touches the sentimental note:

'Fareweel, Land o Moray, I leave theee forever,
Each tie is now broken that knit me to thee';

in the next, he protests at a move to outlaw fishing for finnock on the Lossie:

'The "better class", it seems, may kill
The grouse an deer on moor an hill,
Or feast on salmon, taen at will
Frae loch an river,
While common fowk their wames may fill
Wi skate or liver'.

Frank Sutherland was a high-profile local character. His barber's shops were meeting places for male discussion and gossip and fun. On his death, Scott Skinner published a brief tribute in the *Northern Scot.*

Punchie's Grave

(James 'Punchie' Grant (1793 – 1873) was a shoemaker and a highly skilled fisherman on the Lossie. In Kirkhill Grave yard, close to the river bank, stands an impressive gravestone, raised to Punchie's memory by the 'Gentlemen of Elgin'.)

Wind slowly, dear Lossie, near yonder graveyard,
Wha lang fish'd yer streamlets noo sleeps neath the sward;
Yer wee dancin wavelets yon crackit wa's lave –
The cauld-lookin precincts o poor Punchie's grave.

Oft, oft hath he follow'd thro moorland an lea,
Yer far-windin stream, frae its soorce tae the sea,
Which wimples, an wanders, an winds as o yore,
Tho Punchie, alas! he will stem them no more.

Aa the troots noo wi safety may gambol at will,
In each roarin rapid, in each ripplin rill;
The pikes, tee, wi freedom, may rob aa yer pools,
For Punch, ance their terror, lies low in the mools.

As the sun rose tae welcome the new-born day,
Far doon yer green banks he delightit tae stray
Wi lang crookit hickory an broon-batter'd creel,
By Calcots, Inchbroom, an the deep Coral Peel.

But Punchie's lang wanderin on this side is o'er,
He's cross'd the dark stream tae yon shadowless shore
Whaur strife is unknown, an whaur silence doth reign,
Nae mair tae re-veesit yer streamlets again.

Nae mair will he climb o'er The Rock's dizzy hichts,
Nor muse by The Falls in the lang simmer nichts;
He's left there for ever, nae mair tae return,
Tae foord The Dun Coo nor the dark Lenock Burn.

Nae mair will we see him near auld Kellas Mill,
Nor roostin in Pintie's wee cot on the hill;
Nor hameward returnin past bonnie Manbeen,
As nicht's sable mantle o'ershadows the scene.

He sleeps near the river he ance loed sae weel,
A lang dreamless sleep in a dark narrow biel;
A weird-lookin restin place, lonely an bare –
A stone marks the spot, placed by lovin loons there.

'Twas his wish e'en in death tae be near tae yer stream,
Enshrined amang wild roses, brackens, an breem;
The sons o auld Elgin obeyed his last will –
He rests on yer banks mang the tombs o Kirkhill.

Flow on, gentle Lossie, wind on as before,
Roll seaward yer waters, he heeds not their roar;
Yer wee, wanton wavelets 'God's Acre' may lave,
But touch not the sod that haps poor Punchie's grave.

The Lhanbryd Museum

Hae ye seen Peter's Castle, yon bonnie bit biggin,
The cantiest hoosie on Fife's wide domains?
If nae, pay't a veesit, an dinna need priggin –
It's weel worth the seein, an aa it contains.

It's surroondit wi trappins o Natur's bestowin –
The whun, breem, the bracken, an sweet heather bell,

Frank Sutherland – 'Uncle Peter' (1837–1920)

An near by the door there's a blithe burnie flowin –
A spot whaur a Princess micht fancy tae dwell.

There are few, for rare humour, auld Peter surpasses;
Whan young, for the leddies, he aft got his licks!
Though far up in years he's still fond o the lasses –
It's kittle tae cure an auld horse o ill tricks!

Ye will see aa his fairlies in glorious confusion –
His auld musty pamphlets an kistfu's o lore,
Swords, pistols, an baignets, flint guns in profusion –
An grim-lookin coats o mail, relics o yore.

There's the wheels o the kerrige that bore Robbie Gordon
Across frozen Spynie ae nicht in langsyne;
An twa big baboons frae the banks o the Jordan,
An three wizzen't blethers o Phara's lean kine.

Ye will see Willox' brankst, an the lugs o his cuddie,
The teeth an the tail o a Moray Firth shark,
An also the murderer's club frae Teet Wuddie,
A ghastly memento o dastardly wark.

There's the breeks an the bonnet o Tam o Shanter,
The half o Meg's tail that she tint at the brig;
The deil's stan o bagpipes, complete – bar the chanter –
An Gilpin's identical hat an his wig.

There are twa gowden locks o the ill-used 'Pretender',
Wham fortune betrayed on Culloden's dark field,
The snuff-box an specs o the auld Witch o Endor,
An Bruce's broad claymore, an Wallace's shield.

Stufft warriors are grinnin, wi horrible features,
Mang lang-craigit herons, jackdaws, an curlews,
Stufft polecats, fite foumarts, an ither curst creaturs,
An otters frae Lossie wi fish in their moos.

There are twa horn't oolets – baith quaint aneuch lodgers
That aft woke the echoes o Coxton's grey toor;
Twa dirks an twa sporrans ance owned by the sodgers
Wha perished mang snaw on the bleak Mannoch Moor.

There's a Will-o-the-Wisp, corkit up in a bottle,
Twa witches embalmed frae the deep Order Pot;
An auld greasy rope that Bill Noble did throttle –
The Teet Hill assassin – may's name be forgot!

There's the lang missin link between man an the monkey
A bress, batter'd helmet by foeman ance cleft;
The girth an the tether o Balaam's wise donkey,
 Supposed tae be fand in the auld Moss o Meft!

An lastly, there's ae thing claims special attention,
A droll apparatus I daurna here name;
Gang an see't for yersel – an aloo me tae mention –
Tak some fusky wi ye, or else bide at hame!

An Elgin Holiday

The maist o men an women born
Hae read that 'Man is made tae mourn',
But, quaitly, atween you an me,
Rob's peerless poem's a doonricht lee.
For Solomon – a wiser wit –
Has plainly tauld's, in Holy Writ,

Frank Sutherland – 'Uncle Peter' (1837–1920)

There's time for a'thing neath the sun –
A time for business – an for fun.

This bein so, I here may say,
Last Monday wis oor holiday,
Whan ilka Elgin mither's son
Flang care an business tae the wun,
Leavin, tae gaird oor bonnie toon,
Jock Fyfe, brave Bowsie, an Hugh Broon –
Three Moray loons as true as steel,
Three lanmarks aa respeckit weel.

The Big Kirk Bell was chappin five,
Whan ilka street seemed quite alive
Wi lads an lassies fu o smiles,
Aa drest in fashion's latest styles;
The toon itsel, I thocht, looked prood
Tae see this precious, priceless crood;
Pleased at the lively scene it saw,
Prood that it shelter'd ane an aa.

At six oclock the streets waur swarmin,
An, Lord be thank't, the day was charmin –
The rain that fell for nichts before
Keept aff till aa the fun was oer;
So, young an auld, wi beamin faces,
Set oot in droves tae distant places –
Tae Gairmuch, Cowsea, an the Broch,
Tae mountains, meadow, muir an loch.

I'm tauld that hunners saunter'd sooth,
But thousans swarm'd tae Lossiemooth –
Yon fail-me-never thrivin toon,

Sae *dear* tae ilka Elgin loon;
For there, in sunny auld langsyne,
We scamper'd aff wi heuks an twine
Tae fish, tae dook, an rax oor banes,
Tae gether buckies, dulse, an stanes.
Nae croodit trains ran to an fro –
Plain cairts, wi strae, waur then the go.
Life's early days we'll ne'er forget
Till life's short winter's sun is set.

Some fishin freens flew aff in flocks
Tae spen the day mang Birnie's rocks
Providit for their tedious tasks
Wi rods, reels, creels, an fusky flasks.
O them I heard a watery tale –
But here I draw across the veil!
Nae doot, dear freen, ye'd like tae ken
Whaur I skedaddled? Listen, then!
Braw buskit in my very best,
I sped tae Lossiemooth post haste.

We hired a cab an drove awa–
My wife an bairnies – bless them aa!
But oor turn-oot gaed aa tae pot,
For sic a drive few ever got.
Oor horsie proved a famous flinger,
Wi only three legs an a swinger!
An, privately, 'tween you an me,
Took three oors near tae reach the sea,
For noo an then the blastit thing
Took half-an-oor tae reest an fling,
The wife wi fricht gaun near dementit,
While 'Will' sat lauchin quite contentit!

Frank Sutherland – 'Uncle Peter' (1837–1920)

At length we reached the dear auld port,
In lots o time tae see the sport.

Tae tell o aa the scenes I saw
Wid tak a leisure oor or twa;
But, strange tae say – What dae ye think?
There wis nae ane the waur o drink!
The queerest sicht that catched my eye
Wis flocks o fishermen from Skye,
For mony a loozie, tartaned tyke
Sat jabberin on the lang Sweer Dyke;
An mony a droothy sma ale scorner
Haranguin at the Lazy Corner.

Adjournin tae the herbir moo,
We joined a noisy, fishin crew,
For on it's sea-lashed shattered wa's
Sat Elgin loons as thick as craws.
I bocht twa lines an twa-three hooks
For hangin gairachs, saeths, an flooks,
So Will an I made eager haste
Tae try oor luck amon the rest,
An shortly slew an eel or twa,
Which Will in's poochies stowed awa.

Bait fishin, Frank,'s a hairtless job –
Twad e'en a saint o's patience rob –
So I rowed up the heuks an lines,
An gaed an saw the Stotfield mines;
Syne startit aff across the sans,
Roon whaur the freenly Lichthoose stans,
The bairnies skirlin fu o glee,
Sair puzzled wi yon wond'rous sea,

Poetry of Moray

Bamboozlin me wi bairnish queries
Aboot the boaties an the Skerries!

But Time, that intermeddlin loon,
Wi stealthy steps cam creepin roon;
While *Sol,* ance mair, wi's gowden licht,
Oer western waves sank oot o sicht,
An sable mists began tae fa,
Which stopt the fun o ane an aa;
So, seein decent fowk gaun hame,
We bundled up an did the same.

Oor beastie, duly fed an slockit,
Weel cautioned an securely yokit,
Sprang aff like ony fleggit deer,
Sune leavin Lossie far in rear,
Haltin tae shak its horrid hoch
Whan opposite the ruined loch!
Syne aff we flew ower Spynie hill,
Doon past the Cross o Bishopmill,
On through a clood o stanes an stoor –
Hame in a quarter o an oor!
Safe wi the wife an little anes –
Free o remorse an broken banes.

I've read o Gilpin's famous chase –
But oor's eclipsed that hero's race
Oor freens that left at early morn
Back tae the toon waur safely borne;
Hameward they swarmed frae aa directions,
An deil a ane wi soor reflections.
This feenishes my racy rhyme,
An common sense roars oot – high time!

Lady Middleton (1847 – 1922)

Eliza Maria Willoughby, Lady Middleton, was the eldest child of Sir Alexander Penrose Gordon Cumming of Altyre. She came from a distinguished family of scientists, travellers, and authors. She married Sir Digby Middleton of Wollaton Hall, Nottingham. Her younger brother, William Gordon Cumming, became Baronet. He was at the centre of 'the Baccarat Scandal,' the gambling *cause celebre* involving the Prince of Wales, that ultimately led to the collapse of the Gordon-Cumming fortunes.

Lady Middleton published three volumes of verse: *On the North Wind, Thistledown (*1874), *Ballads* (1878), and *Alasdair Bhan Comyn, The Tragedy of Dunphail* (1889). *The Sandhills of Culbin* arises from the growing interest in the traditional ballads of Scotland, deriving from the work of Scott, Jamieson and others. She was steeped in the legends and history of western Moray. *Alasdair Bhan Comyn* is an extensive work, of book-length, laden with notes, explanations and appendices. It tells the story of the fourteenth century feud between the Comyns and the Randolph family who lived at Darnaway, culminating in the leap of her hero, Alasdair Comyn, across the Findhorn and the final slaughter of the remaining Comyns in the cave at Slaginnan on the Divie. Lady Middleton's literary inspiration seems likely to have been the Ossianic epics of

James Macpherson (1736 – 1796) which, in the mid-nineteenth century, were still immensely popular, despite the long-running debate on their authenticity. The brief extracts below give some sense of her approach.

The Ern, or Findhorn River (from Alastair Bhan Comyn)

Like a bold charger from his stall fresh freed,
Whom not a chiding master's hand and voice
Can check in his exuberance of delight,
But with bound, curvet, plange, and bound again,
Uses less earth than air, and sets more toil
Ten yards to traverse than might pass a mile;
So leaves the Ern her Monadh Liath bed,
And frets through Dulsie, fumes by Ferness fair;
Now gathering force from Divie's added tide,
Where high Relugas sits, tears Logie by,
Spurns the restraint of Sluie's rock-barred bounds,
Where Darnaway's tall oaks are marshalled bold;
Syne gently wearied,'neath the red-rock cliffs
Of lovely Altyre calms to steadier flow,
To sweep and swell through bright Cothall, and meads
(St John's yclept) of joust and tournament;
Then down the laughing Laigh into the sea –
Like the same steed, whose pride, at last bespent,
Calms him to steadier pace and truer speed.

The War (from Alastair Bhan Comyn)

Fierce raged the fight on earth; and fierce in air
The storm, long-lowering, brake; and, rattling, crashed
Opposing clouds, whose thunder-wrack o'er-spreads
The indignant Heavens. Now the levin gleams,

Lady Middleton (1847 – 1922)

And thousand eyeballs wild reflect its glare,
Fraught with deep hate or purpose furyful!
Flash not the dulled claymores; but blood-bedimmed,
They shake red rain athwart the battling airs,
That hurtle, cleft by multitudinous shafts
From twanging bow-strings sped… ah! travailers, what avails
When Doom speaks thundr'ous out down-drooping skies,
And Cormorant Death glides darkling oe'r the foam?

The Sand Hills of Culbin

The Sabbath morn was fair, was fair
And the sky was clear and blue;
And the wee waves glinted in the sun,
As the moulits oe'r them flew.

The lads and lasses all around
Were dighted in their best,
And aa the folk right joyful hailed
Their weekly Sabbath rest.

Fair Culbin lay aneath the sun,
The sweetest spot of all;
And the gardens bloomed wi blossoms bright
Down to the low sea-wall.

The barns and sheds were burstin fu –
For the fields were cleared of corn,
And the wee birds sang a hymn of praise
To the bonnie Sabbath morn.

Oh! Culbin's laird's a fearsome chiel
And no mortal soul fears he!

Poetry of Moray

He scoffs at Word of Heaven's Lord
And wi ill he maks richt free.

'Oh! Can ye leave the cards and dice
An leave the bluid red wine?
An come to the kirk wi me, Kinnayrd,
To pray for my sins – and thine?'

'Get oot get oot – ye silly wife!
What care I for kirk or thee?
An even till the Monday morn
We'll play, my grieve an me!'

'Your grieve, he's going to the kirk,
Where his wife's already gane!
An gif ye'll play this Day, Kinnayrd,
It's sure ye'll play yer lane!'

Oh! Then Kinnayrd leuch loud and lang;
'Ye fule wife, say your say!
For I would play wi the Diel himsel,
Until the Judgment Day!'

There cam a clap o thunder loud,
An a chappin at the door;
And ere they turned, a black, black man
Stood out upon the floor.

The grieve he ran frae out the house,
And the servants followed fast;
But the gudewife she went out and prayed
'Mid the raging northern blast.
'Oh! Where is now the bright blue lift?

Lady Middleton (1847 – 1922)

Dark is the sky and land;
And where are now the gardens fine?
Shrouded in drifting sand!

'The wind is blowing loud, gudeman,
An the sand drifts frae the shore;
I've called ye twice and thrice, gudeman,
An I caa ye now once more.'

'Ye caa again in vain, old wife,
For I'm winning the red, red gold!
An though my hands are hard and strong,
It's burning in my hold.'

And loud and fiercer blew the wind,
And the sand was to the door;
The woman rushed out oer the land,
And wept and cried full sore.
The wind it blew, and the sand it flew,
All through the mirk, mirk night;
But the darksome guest, he played his best
For a soul, by the taper's light.

The morning dawned, the wind went down,
And the sand it blew no more;
For aa the country round about
Was like a vast sea-shore.

And neath the sand that fearfu game
Is played and played always;
For the Deil and Culbin are sitting there
Until the Judgment Day!

William Donaldson (1847 – 1876)

William Donaldson was born in Rathven and attended the parish school. He started work as a shoemaker in Keith but soon moved to work as a printer in Elgin, working for the *Elgin Courier*. Whilst there, he improved his education and spent his leisure time reading widely and writing so effectively that, by the time he was nineteen, he was an established journalist with the paper and had published a book of poems, *The Queen Martyr; and other poems* (1867). His poems are largely imitative of traditional Scottish balladry, but he reveals in some a strongly Radical point of view. The 'birthright' referred to in the refrain of *An Anthem for the Age* is the extension of the franchise achieved, after a long, hard struggle by working people, in the Second Reform Act of 1867. He moved to England and worked as a journalist in Whitehaven and Morley. He died in Leeds at the age of twenty-eight, of opium poisoning.

An Anthem for the Age
Wraiths an bogles aa hae vanished,
Leavin but their names behind;
Mair material thochts hae banished
Phantoms frae the human mind.
Man has learn'd his true position,
Which he daily strives to gain;

William Donaldson (1847 – 1876)

Call it not a dream Elysian,
Nor a longing vague and vain!

Those wha wish to be progressin
Shouldna work without an aim;
We maun get our mental lesson
If we would our birthright claim.

Wad we rise in point o knowledge,
Study mysteries dark as nicht;
Let us seek in nature's college
For a guidin lamp o licht.
Seek it mid the factory's bustle,
Seek it mid the city's din,
An whaur giant branches rustle
Mid the chillin wintry win.

Onward! ever be progressing
Hae a clear an lucid aim;
We maun get our mental lesson
If we would our birthright claim.

We hae minds endow'd wi reason,
Thirstin for a fund o lore;
Let us try in ilka season
To increase the precious store.
We can read by ingle cheery
Whan the snaws o' winter come,
An' the dismal blast sae eerie
Sichs an' whistles roon the lum.

Those wha wish to be progressin
Shoudna work withoot an aim;

We maun get our mental lesson
If we would our birthright claim.
Mighty power to us is given,
Sae we must wi earnest zeal
Strive, as we wad strive for heaven,
To increase the nation's weal.
Hope, like angel blest, is bringin
Tidings o the reign o peace;
Till victorious peals are ringin
Let our labours never cease.

Onward! ever be progressin,
Hae a clear and lucid aim;
We maun get our mental lesson
If we would our birthright claim.

James Simpson (1850 - ?)

Little is known of James Simpson apart from the following: he came originally from Mortlach; he was a member of the staff of the *Elgin and Morayshire Courier;* he wrote under the pen-name of 'Davie Dow'; and, it is thought, he emigrated to America.

The poem is based on Robbie Milne, a well-known local character at the Elgin Market. He and his wife, Meggie, had a little croft high up on the hill above the Buinach Brae on the Dallas road, where he cut peats to sell. He also distilled and sold his own 'dram'. 'Futherer' is a specifically Morayshire word for a carter. The poem gives an interesting picture of an aspect of life in Moray in the second half of the nineteenth century. Robbie Milne died in the Poorhouse in Bishopmill in 1870.

The Kellas Peat-Futherer

Come, listen, an I will sing you a sang
O a carlie wha did tae Kellas belang;
Wha gaitherin o siller wis aye as thrang
As ony bit mannie could be.
Wi his wifie he saw'd an shuir as aits,
He wan his fir an he cuits his peats.

Wi my fa la, etc.
He wore a braid bonnet o bonnie sky blue,
A hammel-spun coat o the verra same hue,
Wi breeks o that like, an queetikins too,
An a plain gabby carle was he;
He'd a coo an twa stirkies that low'd in the byre,
An a marie that caredna for moss or for mire.
Wi my fa la, etc.

He'd a handy wee cairtie o firwiddy rungs,
Wi a strong timmer aixtree, an teugh 'tya' slungs,
An it whistl'd an skreich'd like a thoosan tongues,
An wis heard aye o'er muir an lea;
Besides, he possessed an auld peat barrow,
Wi a coulterless ploo, an a tineless harrow.
Wi my fa la, etc.

Noo Robbie's fail housie stood far up the hill,
Wi few neebors near't; sae he thocht it nae ill
Tae stow in his pantry a canty bit still,
At which he did practise a wee.
An the drappie he brewed was the pure mountain bead –
For the Elgin an Forres fowks liket it gweed.
Wi my fa la, etc.

Whenever the Tuesdays an Fridays cam roun,
The cairtie wis packit wi peats for the toon,
Wi a kaig in the hairt, an his wife on the croon,
An straicht aff tae Elgin gaed he;
While auld towsie collie gat up frae the door,
First yelpit wi joy, then scampert afore.
Wi my fa la, etc.

James Simpson (1850 – ?)

Twa Scots ells in front, ilka brae Rob wad breist,
Oer hillocks an sheughs whaur a wagon micht reist
An brawlie he kent he'd a lifie bit beast,
For a spunkie peat futherer wis he.
An lood wad the aixletree jingle an skreich,
Fae the broom o Manbeen, tae the laich Pittendreich.
Wi my fa la, etc.

Whiles weariet, an langin wi' Meggie tae chat,
Wi the help o a ploud on the tramps up he gat,
An sidlins upon the mare's hurdies he sat,
Syne joggit awa cannily;
An blithely they'd crack o the hauchies an hallows,
An the thrifty peat mosses o Kellas an Dallas.
Wi my fa la, etc.

For win, weet, or weather he caredna a fig
Twas a sair week he cross'dna the Palmerscross Brig,
An doon by the Hospital jirkit fu trig,
As supple as supple could be;
An lood wad he whistle whanever his een
Fell on Maryhill's shrubb'ries an sweet Gallows Green.
Wi my fa la, etc.

O sweet are the crafts aboot Bilboha,
An the bonnie Maine Wood, sae bushy an braw,
An the shaggy Oak Wood – for oor frien kent them a,
For a wanderin bit bodie was he.
The Stappin-Stanes tae, an green Ladyhill.
He kent ilka brae aboot Bishopmill,
Wi my fa la, etc.

Poetry of Moray

He ca'd on Jane Murdoch, the first in the toon,
For she aye keepit something tae warm a 'braw loon':
Or at the 'White Horse', a wee farther doon,
For a pushin bit body wis he;
While Meggie took chairge o the cairt an the beast,
An himsel, bein active, aye managed the rest.
Wi my fa la, etc.

His peats were the best o the black an the broon,
For thrifty an gweed fire weel kent through the toon,
An naebody grudged a sil'er half-croon
For the weel-packit leady tae gie,
For aften they got a bit fir tae the eke,
That held them in licht for a lang winter's week.
Wi my fa la, etc.

When the cairtie wis teem the mare got a rest,
Wi a rip o a sheaf – it suited her best;
The hems were ta'en aff, an the halter made fest
Tae the trams for security;
An blithe wad she nicker 'gweed e'en' tae her fellows,
For brawlie she kent aa the horsies o Kellas.
Wi my fa la, etc.

Oor pair syn wad daunner some fairlies tae spy
Tae gaze on the Muckle Kirk steeple sae high,
Or aiblins, they had some orras tae buy –
Nae hoose frae expense can be free.
Some congou for Meggie – as we micht suppose
Some sneeshin for Robbie, tae tickle his nose.
Wi my fa la, etc.

James Simpson (1850 – ?)

Auld Robbie had nae lithe side tae a brawl
He wis jealous o Gawkie, as weel's Sandy Paul
An yet, when aroused, he wis wicked an bauld,
As ony peat furtherer could be.
In his youth he wis truly a hard-mettled wight,
An I trow but few crossed him withouten a fricht.
Wi my fa la, etc.

He kent Dog Cormie, that prince o the gun
Sure recent events show his wrath is nae fun;
He brings men an muircocks alike tae the grun,
For a sing'lar wild sportsman is he.
Twar better tae get the loons dooked in a puddle,
Than their corduroys bored like a sieve or a riddle.
Wi my fa la, etc.

Havin heard aa the uncos amon the toon's fowk,
An coft aa their orras, an crackit their joke,
Auld Rab got the marie set intae the yoke,
An a lifie bit beastie wis she.
She needit nae wattle tae punish or fricht
Twas eneuch gin she aince got her head tae the heicht.
Wi my fa la, etc.

Thus, week aifter week auld Robbie wis seen,
An a mair hammel carl there couldna weel been;
Though his body wis wither'd his hairt wis aye green,
For a jokie bit bodie wis he.
But he hasna been in auld Elgin for lang,
Nor ane in his place – so here ends my sang.
Wi my fa la, etc.

James McQueen (1852 – 1928)

Born in Edinkillie, where his father had a cartwright's business, James McQueen dabbled in a few occupations before dedicating himself to learning to play the fiddle and becoming an itinerant musician. He bore, in mid-life, a resemblance to the Prince of Wales (later King Edward VII) and made much of that in his busking performance. Nattily dressed, wearing a Glengarry bonnet, he was a popular figure on trains from Wick to Perth and eastward to Aberdeen. The railway companies gave him a pass, enabling him to entertain passengers at stations and on the trains. He sold copies of airs he composed.

He published four books of verse: *Beauties of Morayland* (1895), *The Minstrel of Moray* (1905), *Lays of Findhornside* (1911), and *A Fiddler's Philosophy* (1914). In these volumes he 'sang of the charms of his native county, of the delights of Nature, and of the power of Love'. His obituary proclaims that he was 'happy in the knowledge that his flights [of fancy] excel all others who claim Forres as their town'.

The Morayshire Ploughing Match was sung and recorded by John Macdonald of Pitgaveny, the Singing Molecatcher, whose album, *Scots Ballads, Bothy Songs and Mellodeon Tunes*, was released on Topic Records in 1975.

James McQueen (1852 – 1928)

The Morayshire Ploughing Match

There wis a gey bit stir, I trow,
Among the lads wha caa the ploo;
They met, an were a jolly crew,
Upon the Keam o Duffus.

Frae Drainie an frae Lossie Glen,
Frae Kellas an frae Pluscarden,
The roads were thrang wi brawny men,
Gaun tae the Keam o Duffus.

A hunner ploos, an horses gay,
A wroucht fu bonnie there that day,
An Ballindalloch took the sway
Upon the Keam o Duffus.

The lasses they were buskit braw,
As on that morn they hied awa
Tae see wha wud be chief o aa
Upon the Keam o Duffus.
An, by my certie, some were prood,
When Berryley wis caukit good;
Three ringin cheers were heard fu lood
Upon the Keam o Duffus.

Goodwill an freendship ruled the lot,
An o't some chiels were takin note,
An ye may ken they quickly wrote
Upon the Keam o Duffus.

In by a bittie fae the gate
A gran marquee wis handy set,
In which the wants o a were met
Upon the Keam o Duffus.

The fiddler there struck up a spring –
'Twas Huntly's weel-kent 'Hielan Fling' –
An lads an lasses roon did swing
Upon the Keam o Duffus.

An while the fiddler's airm flied,
An while the winnin names were cried,
They hooed an wheeled wi muckle pride
Upon the Keam o Duffus.

An losh, it wis a blithesome scene
Tae see them shakin hans at e'en;
Ye'd think their joy wid ne'er be deen
Upon the Keam o Duffus.

I ne'er saw sic a happy lot
On ony ither rural spot;
I'll ne'er forget the pleasure o't,
Upon the Keam o Duffus.

Some lads were there wha ploo the main,
As weel as those wha ploo the plain;
I houp they'll aa soon meet again
Upon the Keam o Duffus.

James McQueen (1852 – 1928)

Lossieside

I dream'd o dear auld Moray, when, on my grassy bed,
The smoke o Mons had vanished, and daring foes had
   fled;
I saw my hame at Elgin, whaur fain I'd ever bide
Amid the wealth o grandeur that decks sweet Lossieside!

Lang syne, doon by the Lochie, that winds thro
   Pluscarden,
Near whaur it joins the Lossie, my fond hert swayed
   was then;
And Maggie still is smiling, on yon green broomy braes:
I see her while I'm dreaming, as in the bygane days

Ah! I noo at Elgin, my aa on earth I'd gie
Tae hear the laverock liltin aboon the gowaned lea;
On yon fair meads o Haughland I'd meet my fond
   hert's pride,
And show the love I cherish for dear auld Lossieside

Oh, bring me back to Moray, the land o flower and song!
And let me by the Lossie stray when the days are long;
Enraptured wi fair Maggie, by love my chosen bride,
Bound wi what nought can sever – our pledge on
   Lossieside.

Revd. John Wellwood (1853 - 1919)

John Wellwood was born and educated in Glasgow. His first and only charge, to which he was appointed in 1883, was the parish of Drainie. John Wellwood led the fight, which lasted nearly all his time in Drainie, to have the parish kirk – later to be named St Gerardine's – moved from the existing site, about two miles to the west of the town, to Lossiemouth. He was a much-respected minister with extensive literary gifts as biographer, essayist, poet, and lecturer. Wellwood and his wife lost two of their four sons in the First World War. He was never physically robust. It is said that the loss of his sons hastened his death.

Gouf at Drainie
(Earlier called *The Whin-Whippers.*)
I
As I gaed ower the whinny knowes
Ae windy efterneen,
I saw a very dacent man
Sair angered at a whin.

Aa roon an doon the whin he glowert,
Soliloqueezin on,

Revd. John Wellwood (1853 – 1919)

When suddenly he yerkt his erm,
An gied a lang deep groan.

Noo by him stood a donnered loon
Aboot the age o six,
Wha in his oxter bore a load
O lang an curious sticks;

Frae whilk the man, half-greetin, pu'd
A stick wi an iron tae,
An thrashed that ae bit whin buss
Fu lang I couldna say.

Slow up ayont his shouther an
Swift doon wi fearsome gleam,
The bonnie stickie ca'd awa
As if it gaed by steam.

Twas eerie on the lanely links
Tae hear the constant thud,
An see that very dacent man
Withoot a doot gaen wud.

At orratimes, wi troubled broo,
The daftie keekit in
Tae see whit havoc he had made
On that immortal whin.

An up again the stickie went
An doon again it cam,
An iver as he whipt the whin
He gied the ither damn.

Poetry of Moray

II
Syne frae a wee bit whitey ba
That lay upon the green,
A gey consaitty sort o man
Stept up tae see his frien.

Ahint him was a donnered loon
Aboot the age o six
Wha in his oxter bore a load
O lang an curious sticks.

Thinks I, this seems a kind o game,
Ma man's nae daft ava;
He's spilin whins, but his intent
Is jist tae hit the ba.

'Hard lines,' the blithe newcomer cried,
As if wi pity seized;
'Hard lines,' says he, but yet, I thocht
He lookit unco pleased.

'Ye've played a wheen o niblick shots,
Whit like's yer score?' says he;
The ither, wiping aff the sweit,
Says, 'Forty fae the tee –

'Fifteen for saun an that, an then
As sure as I'm alive,
Jist here in this infernal whin
I've played my twenty-five.'

'Hard lines, man, that ye didna ken
Ye could uplift yer ba

Revd. John Wellwood (1853 – 1919)

An drap it ower yer big saft heid
For jist a fine o twa.

'I'm lyin there at thirty-three;
It's ticht upon ma soul;
Tak oot yer ba an play awa –
Ye'll maybe hauve the hole'.

Fallen in Action

Upon a sunny day
In Elgin town I stray,
When suddenly my feet
Pause in the shining street.

My eyes with tears are dim,
For known of old to him
Were every tree and stone
And all I look upon.

O Elgin town is bright,
All steeped in golden light;
He'll never see it again
In sunshine or in rain.

David J Mackenzie (1855 - 1925)

David MacKenzie was born in Elgin, the son of Thomas MacKenzie of Ladyhill House, architect of Elgin Museum and Drummuir Castle, among many others, and brother of W Marshall MacKenzie, architect of Marischal College, Aberdeen. He was great grandson of William Marshall, the famous composer and fiddler

David Mackenzie was educated at Weston House, Elgin, where Alexander Graham Bell studied and taught, and at Aberdeen Grammar School. He was a distinguished student of Law at Edinburgh University. He then had a very successful career, operating as Sheriff Substitute in various Scottish counties and cities from Shetland to Ayrshire. As a very young man, he started, in Elgin, the literary magazine, *The Grey Friar* (1876), and built up an extensive knowledge of literature, both classical and modern, and contributed to a range of literary and historical magazines. He published a book of essays, *Byways among Books* (1900), which included an account of the life and work of Florence Wilson (c1500 – 1550), the Elgin-born classical scholar and Humanist philosopher. He also wrote a perceptive and appreciative analysis of *The Buke of the Howlat*. His collection of poems (1920) contained many that had been published in *Blackwood's Magazine, The Scots Magazine,* and the *Northern Scot*. He also published a small collection of sonnets to mark the opening of Marischal College.

He retired to Elgin in 1920 and died at Deansford, East High Street, in Bishopmill.

The Old Town-Bell of Elgin

The leaves are thick in the shadows,
The Autumn day is done,
And the old Town-Bell of Elgin
Rings to the falling sun –
Rings to the gathering dark that fills
The woods where the Lossie flows:
From the sleepy meadows of green Oldmills
To the sandy slopes of the Bareflathills
The psalm of evening goes.

The builder drops his trowel,
Glad at that soft command:
The spade is dropped in the furrow,
The pen from the writer's hand.
For the race is run and the day is done
At the sound of the old Town-Bell,
Ringing to-night to the falling sun –
Though some have lost and some have won –
Ringing that 'All is well.'

They hear it by the old Bow Brig
And, over hill and moss,
Beyond the bonnie woods of Mayne
And quiet Palmerscross.
And he who climbs by the Lady Hill
Or drinks at the Mary Well

Will pause to listen, a moment, still
And silent, for all his heart will thrill
At the sound of the old Town-Bell.

There is silver and gold up yonder
Hid in the pillared tower:
Silver of sweet self-sacrifice,
And gold of a sun-bright hour
When lord and labourer, trader and churl,
Threw, as become their lot,
The ring of a man, the brooch of a girl,
The groat of a serf, and the seal of an Earl
Into the melting-pot.

The old Town-Bell of Elgin
More sweetly sounds to me
Than the organs of mighty ministers
Or the clarions of jubilee,
For the murmuring street and river glade,
And even to the heavens above,
Sweet and solemn and unafraid,
It speaks of a peace that the years have made
Holy and full of love.

Ring on, old Bell, in the gloaming,
Your voice is heard afar,
Over the fields that are ripening
Under the evening star.
And further, beyond the hills and the sea,
Are echoes you cannot know,
In hearts that listen and fain would be
By the ruined towers and the green oak tree
And the Lossie's gentle flow.

David J Mackenzie (1855 – 1925)

Ah, many there be that loved it
That will not hear it more,
Whose hearts went out to its music
And the message that it bore.
A message of love and of sweet regret,
The croon of a bird to her nest,
Hope, in tears, as a jewel, set,
The story of all that is past, and yet
A message of perfect rest.

The Laich of Moray

The woods of Inverugie
Look down upon the sea,
And the corn-clad hill of fair Roseisle
Is passing sweet to me
When the sun shines on the water
And the wind blows soft and free
Down by the caves of Covesea
And the well on Hopeman lea.

The rocks of gold are carven
And the white beach shines below,
Where the far-borne sapphire of the sea
Breaks into sighing snow.
You may win at the fall of the tide
To the Cave of the Curse, and, slow,
You may trace the lines, and the woven signs
That only dead men know.

When the hand of Rome had taken
The prey that she might not keep
Her slow, triumphant eagles
Glittered on yonder steep

Poetry of Moray

Where they lit the fires of Ashtaroth –
The fires that will not sleep –
And the bull was slain to Mithras
In the shrine that is hidden deep.

Hoarse is the hungry raven
That wings oe'r Spindle Muir,
And cackling kaes have built their nests
On Spynie's broken floor.
The stars of Sutherland will float
From Duffus' tower no more,
Gone is the shrine of Gerardine
Who prayed by the windy shore.

It is a Priory bell that tolls
From Heldon's woods among,
An answer comes from far Kinloss
Where the three great bells are swung,
Anna, Maria, and Jerome;
And hark! – with golden tongue
Tis the Chanry Kirk of Elgin
Chiming at Evensong.

The deer has drunk in Quarrelwood,
The wolf in Altyre chase;
The moon is up, and great stars light
The sea's unruffled face:
And through the aisles of Pluscarden
The white-cowled brethren pace,
And throw them down by the Holy Rood,
Praying for Heaven's grace.

David J Mackenzie (1855 – 1925)

A land of many memories,
A land whose gardens smile,
Whose harvest fields lie in the sun
For many a golden mile.
I look on the Laich of Moray
Dreaming a little while,
For the past is full of faces,
And Fancy will beguile.

May M Dawson (1860 – 1947)

May Dawson was the daughter of Alexander Thomson, farmer at Corskie, Garmouth. A pupil at Milne's Institution, Fochabers, she was engaged to Major Allan Wilson, of Fochabers (1858 –1893), hero of the Shangani Patrol, massacred during the Matabele Wars in Northern Rhodesia. In 1896, May married James Dawson, also a former pupil at Milne's, who had been a close friend of Allan Wilson. Dawson was a meat trader in Northern Rhodesia, a friend of Cecil Rhodes, and a significant figure in the development of the Colony. May joined her husband in Bulawayo, but, in 1905, left him to return to live at The Brae, Garmouth, with their only child, Ronald. She had, allegedly, been the victim of her husband's abuse.

In 1901, she had published *The Veldt and the Heather, Memories of home and sketches of life in the land of Lobengula*. On returning home, she continued to write poetry and little 'sketches', mainly for the *Northern Scot*. James Dawson shot himself in 1921.

In the aftermath of the First World War, May Dawson published a book of poems, entitled *Tinkers Twa in Peace and War* (no date, but, probably, post 1925). Her purpose was to present the Travelling folk as human beings and recognize their contribution in the War.

May M Dawson (1860 – 1947)

The Tinker's Trek

It's the screich o day – I maun awa,
My caravan's at the door,
Wi jinglin bells on my horse's reins,
An my tins an brooms in store;
It's the gowden, hairty hairvest time,
An the days are drawin in,
An it's nae lang time frae dawn tae dark –
I maun haste the road tae win.

Wi my tattie-pot an my hodden grey
I envy nae a prince,
For a millionaire can only wear
Ae set o duds at aince;
I pitch my tent inside the wood,
An tether my horse to feed,
While I shouther my tins to the cottars' hames
An speer what pans they need:
'Will ye buy a brander,
A toaster or a stander,
A juggie for the bairn,
Or a fine milk pail?'

A rabbit bolts frae a roadside hole,
There's a craw on the birken tree,
But the tinker is aye aboot their feet,
An kin to them baith, you see;
An the thocht comes ower me, laddie,
As I jog alang my way,
I may meet you, wi your bagpipes braw,
By the woodside ony day.

Then you'll start an tune your chanter fine,
An you'll gar the fir woods ring
Wi 'The Reel o Tullochgorum'
Or 'The Marquis' Hielan Fling',
Syne I'll rest my back by a mossy bank,
An you'll come an sit by me,
An I'll sing to you, 'Where the Gadie rins
At the back o Benachie'.

Mary Symon (1863 - 1938)

Mary Symon was born in Dufftown, the elder daughter of John Symon, proprietor of the family saddler's business. Her mother was a farmer's daughter from Drywells in the Cabrach. After early education at Mortlach School, Symon was sent to the Edinburgh Institute for Young Ladies (later, to become Edinburgh Ladies' College). On leaving school, she returned to Dufftown and undertook the Lady Literate in Arts (LLA), a qualification offered by correspondence by the University of St Andrews in the decade or so before women were admitted to degree courses in Scotland's universities. In 1889, her father, now Provost of Dufftown, purchased Pittyvaich House, which was Mary Symon's home until her death in 1938.

Mary Symon's work in verse and prose had, from the 1890s, appeared in a variety of publications, including *The Scots Magazine*, *New Century Review* and the *Aberdeen Journal* when, in February 1916, *The Glen's Muster Roll: the Dominie Loquitur* was published in *Aberdeen University Review*.

This is a rich, multi-layered poem. It has been described, by Colin Milton, as 'perhaps the finest vernacular elegy to come out of the Great War'. No other poem evokes so effectively the sense of the loss to a community of a whole generation. Symon's stroke of genius is in the creation of the voice of the Dominie, whose use of the Doric is a binding force in the community. He has taught every one of the young men whose names make up the Muster Roll. The Dominie remembers and reflects on the fate of eight of his loons.

In the final stanza the Dominie has a hellish vision of the dead and the wounded returning to the school room:

> 'Ye're back fae Aisne an Marne an Meuse, Ypres an Festubert:
> Ye're back on weary bleedin feet – you, you that danced an ran –
> For every lauchin loon I kent I see a hell-scarred man.'

The closing lines express the helplessness and the hopelessness of the Dominie, the representative of the establishment that authorised the War, confronted by the ultimate question posed by his ghostly visitors: 'Ah, Maister, tell's fit aa this means'. His only reply is in the 'bairns' words' that they used to use in response to his questions on The Rule of Three or Latin declensions or the Catechism:

> 'I dinna ken, I dinna ken. Fa does, oh Loons o Mine?'

This poem instantly struck a chord in the hearts and minds of the people of the North-East. It was much reprinted and anthologised and it, along with a handful of other poems, most of them monologues with distinctive and beautifully realised voices, established Mary Symon's reputation as a poet of national importance.

In those days the use of vernacular Scots was seriously under threat. Mary Symon was determined to 'remove from the minds of simple people that only vulgar people speak the Doric' and 'to convince the Scottish Education Department that Scots must be taught in schools or at least be encouraged

Mary Symon (1863 - 1938)

to be read in the classroom'.

For a long time, she resisted friends' urging to seek wider publication. In 1933, when her collection of poems, *Deveron Days*, appeared, published by Wyllie of Aberdeen, it sold out within a week. It was immediately reprinted and sold out again. A second edition with additional poems was published in 1938.

Her obituarist, in the *Dufftown News* of 4 June 1938, writes:

> 'Mary Symon was a woman of extraordinarily wide culture, familiar with several languages, and a keen and discerning student of literature, philosophy and life. Her conversation was a joy and a constant delight, full of wisdom, kindness and humour ... She was never happier than when acting as hostess to a party of her friends. On one memorable day three Fellows of the Royal Society sat together at her table and she revelled in the keen interplay of their brains, in which she took the competent part...Her native countryside and its people and customs she loved with a passionate devotion. Her love of Scotland was no mere artistic sentiment but her creed, and it was that sincerity, projected into her poetry and her conversation, that made her words memorable'.

The Soldier's Cairn

Gie me a hill wi the heather on't,
An a reid sun drappin doon,
Or the mists o the mornin risin saft
Wi the reek owre a wee grey toon.
Gie me a howe by the lang Glen road,
For it's there 'mang the whin an fern

Poetry of Moray

(D'ye mind on't, Will? Are ye hearin, Dod?)
That we're biggin the Soldiers' Cairn.

Far awa is the Flanders land
Wi fremmit France atween,
But mony a howe o them baith the day
Has a hap o the Gordon green;
It's them we kent that's lyin there,
An it's nae wi stane or airn,
But wi brakin herts, an mem'ries sair
That we're biggin the Soldiers' Cairn.

Doon, laich doon the Dullan sings
An I ken o an aul sauch tree,
Where a wee loon's wahnie's hingin yet
That's dead in Picardy.
An ilka win fae the Conval's broo
Bends aye the buss o ern,
Where aince he fettled a name that noo
I'll read on the Soldiers' Cairn.

Oh! Build it fine an build it fair,
Till it leaps to the moorland sky
More, more than death is symbolled there,
Than tears or triumphs by.
There's the Dream Divine of a starward way
Oor laggard feet would learn,
It's a new earth's corner-stone we'd lay
As we fashion the Soldiers' Cairn.

Lads in your plaidies lyin still,
In lands we'll never see,
This lanely cairn on a hameland hill

Mary Symon (1863 - 1938)

Is aa that oor love can dee;
An fine an braw we'll mak it aa,
But oh, my Bairn, my Bairn,
It's a cradle's croon that'll aye blaw doon
To me fae the Soldiers' Cairn.

The Wag-At-The-Wa

Aul sconface we ca'ed it, hairst-bap an the like
Aa pictered wi hoosies, an a bike,
Wi dosses o roses meanderin roon
Oh! A plenishin gran, baith for sicht an for soun.
The but-the-hoose cheeper had muntins nae mous,
The lever could tell's fan tae yoke an tae lowse,
O the aul kitchey caser we couldna weel blaw,
But losh! we wis prood o oor Wag-at-the-wa.

It briested ye straucht as ye opened the door;
Maybe ae 'oor ahin, maybe twa-three afore.
'Bit fiech! fat o that?' the aul man would say,
'A college curriculum's oor time o day!'
An tappin his mullie, he'd stot awa ben,
'Noo, ye see, lads, the han's at the hauf aifter ten,
An it's new chappit ane – Weel, Greenwich an me
Positeevely can state – *it's a quarter fae three!*
Ay! Logic, Algebra – ye sair nott them aa
When ye set oot to bothom oor Wag-at-the-wa.

The fun that we made ot! The lauchs that we got!
I could tell them aa yet, though the greet's in my throat.
. . . Aul chap, on yir kopje (or is't a karoo?),
Div ye min the Eel-even, when some ane got fou?
When the reel 'naith the rafters was ill for his queet,
But he'd dance, he could swear, the backstep on a peat;

Poetry of Moray

When wi little persuasion he sang to the cat,
An tellt the stuffed oolet jist aa fat was fat;
But to ken foo't aa ended, an fa bested fa –
Weel, I'd need to *sub poena* the Wag-at-the-wa.

An Jean, ye're awa amon bleckies to bide!
Ye're rich an ye're gran, an 'my lady' beside;
But fyles, wi yir fine things an fair things aa roon,
Will yer een maybe fill, an yir heart gie a stoon?
As the aul days come back; the lad at the door,
An the 'weeshtin', till owre the stair-head comes a snore.
Syne, oh! Lassie, syne – but I winna say mair –
Aa the glamour an glory o life met ye there,
An Heaven cam gey near to the wearyfu twa
That kissed their first kiss 'naith the Wag-at-the-wa.

Ay, we're aa scattered noo, but it's aye tickin on
Ye hear't at the dykeside, ye hear't up the loan
Ye hear't – divn't ye, lad? By the lang lippin seas
That soom by yir doorcheek at the Antipodes.
An Tam, wi yir tackets on Ottawa's steep,
What is't that comes back when ye canna get sleep?
Jist the croon o a burn in a far-awa glen,
The clink o a churn, or a fit comin ben,
An in laich obligato, the lift an the fa,
The sab an the sang o a Wag-at-the-wa.

Day's aifter ilk dawnin an nicht aifter e'en;
But there's nae steppin back owre the gait we hae gane;
An Fate winna huckster, or tell fat she'd hae
To lan me a loon again, doon the aul brae –
Wi the lang road afore; wad I bide? Wad I gang?
Ah! me! I ken noo, but the kennins taen lang.

Mary Symon (1863 - 1938)

... Though kind's been the farin, an crowned the quest,
For the bit that's gane by me, I'd swap aa the rest.
The braw beild is yonder I set oot tae win,
An 'Ichabod''s up or the door I'm weel in.
There was sun on the summit I ettled to speel,
But it's mirk noo I'm up, an I'm weary as weel.
What's glory? What's gold? A quate heart's worth them aa,
An I left mine langsyne by a Wag-at-the-wa.

The Glen's Muster-Roll
The Dominie Loquitur:-
Hing't up aside the chumley-cheek, the aul glen's Muster Roll,
Aa names we ken fae hut an haa, fae Penang to the Pole,
An speir na gin I'm prood o't – losh! coont them line by line,
Near han a hunner fechtin men, an they aa were Loons o Mine.

Aa mine. It's jist like yesterday they sat there raw on raw,
Some tyaavin wi the 'Rule o Three', some widin throu 'Mensa';
The map o Asia's shoggly yet faur Dysie's sheemach head
Gaed cleeter-clatter aa the time the carritches was said.
'A limb,' his greetin granny swore, 'the aul deil's very limb',
But Dysie's deid and drooned lang syne; the *Cressy* coffined him.
'Man guns upon the fore barbette!'... What's that to me an you?
Here's moss an burn, the skailin kirk, aul Kissack beddin's soo.
It's Peace, it's Hame – but owre the Ben the coastal search

lights shine,
And we ken that Britain's bastions mean – that sailor
Loon o Mine.

The muirlan's lang, the muirlan's wide, an fa says 'ships'
or 'sea'?
But the tang o saut that's in wir bleed has puzzled mair
than me.
There's Sandy wi' the birstled shins, faur think ye he's
the day?
Oot where the hawser's tuggin taut in the surf o
Suvla Bay;
An owre the spurs o Chanak Bahr gaed twa lang
stilpert chiels,
I think o flappin butteries yet or weyvin powets' creels
Exiles on far Australian plains – but the Lord's
ain boomerang
'S the Highland heart that's aye for hame, hooever far
it gang;
An the winds that wail owre Anzac an requiem Lone Pine
Are nae jist aa for stranger kin, for some were
Loons o Mine.

They're comin hame in twas an threes; there's
Tam fae Singapore -
Yon's his, the string o buckie-beads abeen the aumry door
An Dick Macleod, his sanshach sel
(Guidsake, a bombardier!)
I see them yet ae summer day come hodgin but the fleer:
'Please, sir' (a habber an a hoast), 'Please, sir'
(a gasp, a gulp, Syne wi a rush)
'Please – sir – can – we – win – oot – to droon – a – fulp?'
... Hi, Rover, here, lad! Ay, that's him, the fulp they didna

Mary Symon (1863 - 1938)

droon,
But Tam – puir Tam lies cauld an stiff on some grey
 Belgian dune,
An the *Via Dolorosa*'s there, faur a wee bit cutty quine
Stans lookin doon a teem hill road for a sojer Loon o
 Mine.

Fa's neist? The Gaup – A Gordon wi the 'Bydand'
 on his broo,
Nae murlacks dreetlin fae his pooch or owre his
 grauvit noo,
Nae word o groff-write trackies on the 'Four best
ways to fooge'
He steed his grun an something mair, they tell me,
 oot at Hooge.
But owre the dyke I'm hearin yet: 'Lads, fa's on for
 a swap?
A lang sook o a pandrop for the sense o *verbum sap*.
Fack's death, I tried to min on't – here's my gairten
 wi the knot
But – bizz ! a dhubrack loupit as I passed the muckle pot'.
…Ay, ye didna ken the classics, never heard o a co-sine,
But here's my aul lum aff tae ye, dear gowkit Loon o Mine.

They're handin oot the haloes, an three's come to the glen
There's Jeemack taen his Sam Browne to his mither's but
 an ben.
Ay, they caa me 'Blawin Beelie,' but I never crawed
 sae crouse
As the day they gaed the V.C to my *filius nullius*.
But he winna sit 'Receptions' nor keep on his aureole,
Aa he says is 'Dinna haiver, jist rax owre the Bogie Roll'.
An the Duke an's dother shook his han an speirt aboot

    his kin.
'Old family, yes; here sin the Flood,' I smairtly chippit in.
(Fiech! Noah's? Na – we'd ane wirsels, ye ken, in '29.)
I'm nae the man tae stan an hear them lichtlie
    Loon o Mine.

Wir Lairdie. That's his mither in her doos-neck silk
    gaun by,
The podduck, so she tells me, 's haudin up the H.L.I.
An he's stanin owre his middle in the Flanders'
    clort an dub,
Him that eese't to scent his hanky, an speak o's
    mornin 'tub'.
The Manse loon's dellin divots on the weary road to Lille,
An he canna flype his stockins, cause they hinna
    tae nor heel.
Sennelager's gotten Davie – aa moo fae lug tae lug -
An the Kaiser's kyaak, he's writin, 'll neither ryve nor rug,
'But mind ye' (so he post-cards), 'I'm already owre the
    Rhine.'
Ay, there's nae a wanworth o them, though they werena
    loons o Mine.

…You – Robbie. Memory pictures: Front bench, a
    curly pow,
A chappit hannie grippin ticht a Homer men't wi' tow
The lave aa scrammelin near him, like bummies roon a
    bike.
'Fat's this?' 'Fat's that?' He'd tell them aa – ay, speir
    they fat they like.
My hill-foot lad! Aa sowl an brain fae's bonnet to
    his beets,
A 'Fullarton' *in posse*, nae the first fun fowin peats.

Mary Symon (1863 - 1938)

… An I see a blithe young Bajan gang whistlin
    doon the brae,
An I hear a wistful Paladin his patriot credo say.
An noo, an noo I'm waitin till a puir thing hirples hame,
Ay, 't's the Valley o the Shadow, nae the mountain heichts
    o Fame.
An where's the nimble nostrum, the dogma fair and fine,
To still the ruggin heart I hae for you, oh, Loon o Mine?

My Loons, my Loons! Yon winnock gets the settin sun
    the same,
Here's sklates and skailies, ilka dask aa futtled wi' a name.
An as I sit a vision comes: Ye're troopin in aince mair,
Ye're back fae Aisne an Marne an Meuse, Ypres
    an Festubert;
Ye're back on weary bleedin feet – you, you that
    danced an ran –
For every lauchin loon I kent I see a hell-scarred man.
Not mine but yours to question now! You lift
    unhappy eyes
'Ah, Maister, tell's fat aa this means.' And I, ye thocht
    sae wise,
Maun answer wi the bairn words ye said tae me langsyne:
'I dinna ken, I dinna ken.' Fa does, oh, Loons o Mine?

(Sennelager: a German prisoner-of-war camp.
'Fullarton': a University bursary.)

Nannie Katharin Wells (1875 – 1963)

Nannie Katharin Wells (nee Smith) was born, one of six children, in 1875 in Banffshire, where her father was Rector of Fordyce Academy until, in 1880, he was appointed Rector of Milne's Institution, Fochabers. She was educated at Milne's Institution and Aberdeen University and, like many of her contemporaries, disqualified by her sex from graduating, took an LLA (Lady Literate in Arts) from St Andrews University. In 1901, she married, in Bellie Parish Church, Bernard Norman Wells, a solicitor from Ipswich, and moved to England. She became well-known as a political activist, journalist, novelist, and poet.

In 1910, the family (there were now three sons) was settled in Barnard Castle in County Durham. She became an outstanding advocate for women's suffrage – 'the equal of any opponent, male or female, in a debate on the issue', according to the press.

After the First World War, she moved with her family to Oxford before she returned to Scotland and threw herself wholeheartedly into politics. By 1929, she was depute secretary of the newly formed Scottish National Party. She became a close friend of CM Grieve (Hugh MacDiarmid) and was drawn into the Edinburgh literary circle which included such writers as Leslie Mitchell (Lewis Grassic Gibbon), Neil Gunn,

Nannie Katharin Wells (1875 – 1963)

Eric Linklater, Helen Cruikshank, Marion Angus, and Edwin Muir.

In her novel, *Diverse Roads*, published in 1932, and in her extensive journalistic writings, she pursues her aim to energise 'rheumaticky minds with modern electric shock equipment'.

She took to writing poetry late and published two volumes: *Twentieth Century Mother and other poems* (1952) and *The Golden Eagle* (1958). The nationalist strain is strong – as is the sentimental. In *A Prayer* she writes:

> 'God, give us the grace to hate
> our unemancipated state,
> and to wipe from Scotland's face
> her intellectual disgrace'.

She died in Oxford and was buried, beside her family, at Kinloss Abbey.

To the Twentieth-Century Mother

Let in the day of his darkness,
the day of his darkness and light,
leaving behind
the shadow-bright, film-reel hardness
of your day and kind.

Watch him lean
on the pillar that must fall
in the unrehearsed scene
beyond your call;
the inevitable, necessary fumble
in the under-water vault;
the pre-ordained stumble
into your darling fault;

Nothing of you can atone
for this your flesh and your bone;
nothing you have can buy
him proud immunity;
you must even beware
of too much prayer –
(so much prayer is wishing and wanting
And worship-scanting)
It is required of the mature
to endure – to remember –
to learn again to die, drowned deep under
the waters of love, the rivers of surrender.

Oh mad generosity of women, wine-deep in love.
Ripeness of sun in their veins, glowing and growing,
cool-sweet flesh, living and giving full-tide stillness,
sailing secure on the vigour, the heart-pulse of man,
ringing the fortified bounds of the globe,
Bulges in his blood, breath of supremacy,
lighting the peaks, sky-taking, moon-hooking,
    star-shooting,
sinking slow somersaults deep down under
the sea; – untamed, unsounded;
Oh shuddering, never-ending surrender
of women, sea-deep in love.

Badenach

The wind from Dava Moor sweeps Findhorn Bay
– wind from the west is wild and bends the trees
like people on their knees –
It sweeps the Laigh o Moray, whirls the Spey
up into floods that tear the red cliffs down;

Nannie Katharin Wells (1875 – 1963)

Vessel of wrath attacks the ships at sea
careless of goods and gear and men that drown
unpitied;
Sudden it drops!
Torrents of rain fill up the thirsty lochs
Torridon, Rannoch, Vennachar, Ness and Tay;
Swift the rain stops!
Bright windless day endears
the cruel cliff-face, the lifting peak;
the hills of God shine with our human tears.

It is our stinging privilege –
we are compelled to seek
life at its keenest quick, its hardest edge;
this dialectic we can not escape…
this shape of land our true soul-body shape.

The Stannin Stanes
The Stannin Stanes
The years rise up and stand around me in a circle,
closing me in:
like Stannin Stanes they look to every airt,
possess sun, moon, and stars
and are possessed, living in living earth
as in the music of the resounding sky
ringing with words –
gods', men's, and birds –
the theme emerging still
in variations of unending skill.
And the Stanes, seeming to stand,
dance with the planet, the solar round, the tribal

dance of the universal,
closing me in,
leaving me free to thread my private way
between them, night and day.

JM Caie (1878 – 1949)

John Morrison Caie was born in Durris in Kincardineshire and brought up on the Enzie, the broad stretch of land that rises from the sea at Portgordon to the Hill of Aultmore, near Keith. His father was the parish minister. Educated at Milne's Institution and later at the University of Aberdeen, he had a deep and lifelong interest in and commitment to the farming life. He graduated with degrees of MA and Bachelor of Law before taking a BSc in Agriculture. He worked in Ireland and at the East of Scotland College of Agriculture, before moving to the Department of Agriculture for Scotland, where he remained until his retirement, reaching the position of Deputy Secretary, with particular responsibility for education and research.

Caie's poetry was published, from his University days, in *Alma Mater*, *Aberdeen University Review*, the *Press and Journal*, and the *Scots Magazine*. He published two books of poems – *The Kindly North* (1934) and *'Twixt Hills and Sea* (1939). In his best work, he makes skilled use of poetic form and is a master of his North-East tongue. His work is rooted in the Enzie. It can be sharply realistic, comic, wry, gently reminiscent but is not sentimental – 'sair wark's nae easy', he insists, and 'it's gey an sair tae be strippit, flypit, bare, efter trauchlin in the yird for fifty year'. There is no touch of the Kailyard in his poetry. *The Puddock* is still taught and learnt in schools throughout Scotland, and is arguably one of the best known of poems in Scots or Doric.

JM Caie was awarded an Honorary LLD from the University of Aberdeen in 1945.

The Enzie

I forgaithered ae day wi an Enzie loon,
An, weel-a-wat, there was twa o's;
Sae doon we sat for a wee bit crack,
An there we bade, an we spak an we spak
Nae eyn there was tae the jaw o's;
An the names, as the pairis we wanered roon,
Had a lilt an a sough like a lang-kent tune:

'There's Birkenbush an Sauchenbush, the Smerick
    an Slackheid –
The bonnie ferms are there yet, but the aul folk
    maun be deid –
Portgordon an Port Tannachy, Cowfurrach, an Broadley,
An for Pharpar an Abana gie's the Tynet an the Spey.

There's Dallachy an Gollachy, Wellheads an Allalath,
The sandy road tae Clochan, an Whiteash's strait
    wee path;
There's Auchenreath, Glasterim, Auchenhalrig, an Oxhill,
An Chapelford an Tullochmoss, the Holl, the Breem,
    the Mill.

There's Muir o Homie, Cairnfield, Preshome an
    Cuttlebrae,
The big dark wids o Fochabers, St. Ninians, Auchentae,

JM Caie (1878 – 1949)

The Cockhat Kirk (a queer name thon!), an Oran
    an Howcore,
An up the brae there's Starryhaugh, Scraphard
    an syne Aultmore.'

Aa curnie daft, aul-farrant wirds tae them that doesna ken,
But something mair, oh, something mair, tae twa
    auld Enzie men.

The Auld Ploo Man

It's a bonny-lyin craftie, fine an lythe ayont the hill,
An the hoose, gin it were snoddit up, wad dee;
Ma ee was on't for lang, but things has aa gane vrang
An the hoosie an the craft are nae for me.

Na, na, I'm nae compleenin, though auld age is
    drawin on
An I be tae steyter doon the brae ma lane;
But I've vrocht sin I was twal in sun an rain an caul,
An I'd likit weel a placie o min ain.

Ay, a couthy craft like thon wad jist hae ser't the
    wife an me,
We'd hae keepit twa-three kye an hens an swine;
We'd hae tyaav'd awa thegither, aye helpin ane anither
Hoot, ay the place wad jist hae shuitit fine.

Ach, but fat's the eese o thinkin on the thing I canna hae,
For noo I've neither wife nor son nor gear?
Still an on, it's gey an sair tae be strippit, flypit, bare
Efter trauchlin in the yird for fifty year.

The loon we had but ane he was a shortsome wee bit ted;
Tae his mither he'd nae marra in the lan;
Syne the mester at the squeel thocht him unco gleg as
    weel
An begood tae tak the laddie by the han.

'Twas the dominie that gar't us mak a scholar o the loon,
Though I dinna mean tae say that we were sweir;
Na, na, we baith were fain, but the bawbees we'd tae hain –
Dod, we'd little claes or kitchy mony a year.

We sent him til the college wi the siller we'd laid by;
It was jimp eneuch, but that made little odds,
For, awat, the bairn got on; I've a lot of beuks he won
Wi airms an mottoes stampit on the brods.

Syne a day cam fan his mither an the dominie set aff
Tae see the laddie getting his degree;
That's his picter wi his hood; fegs, his mither was fell
    prood
Fan he got it taen and brocht it hame tae me.

He was aye a thochtfu cratur, an he'd fairly set his hert
On plenishin a craft or wee bit ferm;
Gin ma laddie had been here I wadna nott tae speir
For the ingyaun o the craftie at the term.

But ma schemes, like plenty ither fowk's, have aa gane sair
    agley,
For e'er he'd got a start or taen his stance,
The war cam on, an syne of coorse he be tae jine,
An noo he's beeried hine awa in France.

JM Caie (1878 – 1949)

His mither never cower't it; she was jist aa kin o tint,
Like a body steppin oot intae the mirk;
She'd nae fushion left ava, for she dwined an pined awa,
An she's happit in the mools ahin the kirk.

Ah, weel, fat maun be maun be, an there's naething for't but thole,
Though it's longsome in the forenicht aa yer lane;
Ye've waefu, waukin dreams fan yer wardle's aa in leems,
But I'll need awa an yoke – it's chappit ane.

I'm fley'd I maybe winna hae the second pair for lang,
For I wasna swack eneuch tae tak the cowt;
I ken fat's comin neist – I maun caa the orra beast,
Or gyang an help the byllie wi the nowt.

It'll fairly be a come-doon fan I think upon ma craft,
But a sma affair compared wi aa the lave;
An mony a chiel has trod that verra samen road
An like me gane quately hirplin til his grave.

Sair Wark's Nae Easy

Doon at Nether Dallachy
There's neither watch nor knock,
But denner time an supper time,
An aye yoke, yoke.

It's hingin in, aye hingin in,
Aa day fae sax tae sax,
The deil a meenit div ye get
Tae gie yersel a rax

In winter time it's plooin ley,
Or anse it's caain muck
Or neeps tae serve the byllie's nowt,
Or thrashin a bit ruck.

The stem-mull at a neep'rin toon
Is shortsome, but it's sair
A fraucht o barley's nae that licht
Tae shouther up a stair.

But files there'll be a bonny ploy
Fan lassies tramp the soo,
An filies tae an anterin dram
For sweelin doon the stew.

Syne roon again comes shaavin time
Wi grubber, roller, harra,
Tae haud fowk oot o langer, dod,
The hairst's its only marra.

Ye're skilpin on throu steens an stoor
Until ye've fir't yer feet,
An aye the grieve is girnin, 'Jock,
Hing in, ye dozy breet.'

Syne birze an scrap an birze again,
Fan neeps come tae the hyow;
Yon foreman chiel, he's sic a de'il
For hashin, hashin throu.

Yer back may crack, it doesna mak,
Ye be tae ca awa

JM Caie (1878 – 1949)

Sae fa's wyte is't ye canna wale
The big anes fae the sma?

An neist ye're ootbye at the moss
Tae cast the winter's peat;
A fusome, clorty business gin
The lair be saft an weet.

Ye've syne the hey tae tak aboot,
An gin the wither's shoory
It's nesty, scuttery kin o wark,
An fan it's dry it's stoory.

The hairst! My certies, thon's the job
Tae gar ye pech an swyte,
An gin ye fa ahin the lave
The grieve gyangs fairly gyte.

It's fine, nae doot, tae hurl aboot
For him that ca's the reaper,
But nae sae fine tae bin an stook
Aside a forcey neiper.

Fae morn tae nicht there's nae devaal
Fae trauchlin aye an tyaavin,
Ye've hardly time tae claw yersel
Fan yoky wi a yaavin.

It's boo an lift an boo again
Until ye're like tae drap,
An maybe files ye'll hae tae scythe
A laid an tousled crap.

A weel, at lang length clyak comes,
Ye've stook't the hinmost rig;
The warst ot's bye, but still an on
It's aa tae fork an big.
There's eident days, an forenichts tee
Aneath a muckle meen
Afore ye've gotten winter an
Anither hairst is deen.

Dod, man, it's gran tae see the rucks
Straucht stanin an weel-shapit:
Ye've deen yer darg an there it is
Aa thackit braw an rapit.

But hear the grieve: 'Ye glaikit gype,
There's nae time tae be lost;
Awa an get the tatties up
An happit fae the frost'.

Or lang ye're at the ploo again,
Sae roon the sizzens rin,
An aye by tearin oot the life
Ye try tae haud it in.

Doon at Nether Dallachy
There's neither watch nor knock,
But denner time an supper time,
An aye yoke, yoke.

The Puddock
A puddock sat by the lochan's brim,
An he thocht there was never a puddock like him.

JM Caie (1878 – 1949)

He sat on his hurdies, he waggled his legs,
An cockit his heid as he glowered throu the seggs.
The bigsy wee cratur was feelin that prood
He gabit his mou an he crakit oot lood :
'Gin ye'd aa like tae see a richt puddock,' quo he,
'Ye'll never, I'll sweer, get a better nor me.
I've fem'lies an wives an a weel-plenished hame,
Wi drink for my thrapple an meat for my wame.
The lasses aye thocht me a fine strappin chiel,
An I ken I'm a rale bonny singer as weel.
I'm nae gaun tae blaw, but th' truth I maun tell
I believe I'm the verra MacPuddock himself …'

A heron was hungry an needin tae sup,
Sae he nabbit th' puddock and gollup't him up;
Syne rankled his feathers: 'A peer thing', quo he,
'But – puddocks is nae fat they eesed tae be'.

Gey Likely – 1707
Sic a stramash,
Sic a dirdin an steer
Rase in peer Scotlan
That terrible year.
The country was conach'd,
Aathing gaed vrang;
That was the eyn
O wir 'auld sang'.

On farm an craft the fowk gaed daft,
The peats grew clorty, weet an saft,
The aits wi smuts they grew aa black,
The deil a stack there was tae thack,
The barley wadna yield its bree

(A sair affair for you an me),
The feint a hen wad lay its eggs,
An ilka shilt got cleekit legs.
Tatties aa were coorse an scabbit,
Ne'er a snare wad haud a rabbit;
Kye gaed dry as Irish stirks,
Mice took refuge in the kirks.
Sheep wi scrapie tint their oo,
Fusky wadna fill ye fu.
The neeps were fozy, cankert, wizent,
The wallies failed, the bowies gizent,
The sicht o grozerts fleggit cocks,
The hans fell aff the echt-day knocks.
Great rottans ran aboot the fleers
An golochs crawled on aa the cheers.
The girss nae mair the dew wad kep,
An bees forhooiet ilka skep.
The fulpie wadna chase his tail,
The halflin wadna sup his kail,
The byllie wadna kiss the deem,
For herts were caul an girnals teem.

Sic ferlies as had ne'er been seen
Gart moudieworts tae blink their een.
But half the tribbles that befell
'Twad fairly gar me grue to tell.

The country was conach'd,
Aathing gaed vrang;
That was the eyn
O wir 'auld sang'.

Andrew Young (1885-1971)

Andrew Young was born on 29 April 1885 at the Highland Railway Station in Elgin, the youngest of four children of the stationmaster. Within a few years, the family moved to Edinburgh. Young attended the Royal High School and then prepared for the ministry at New College, Edinburgh. After the first World War, during which he served as a Chaplain in France, Young moved to a Presbyterian ministry near Brighton. During the 1920s and 1930s, he wrote a succession of slim volumes of verse and some poetic religious drama. In 1939, he converted to the Church of England and, in 1941, obtained the parish of Stonegate, Sussex, where he remained until his retirement in 1959. He was made a canon of Chichester Cathedral in 1947 and, following his retirement, he moved to Yapton to be nearer the Cathedral. Young enjoyed being an English vicar, but he remained distinctively Scottish. He never lost his Scottish accent. He said of the town of his birth:

> 'Doctor Johnson had a poor opinion of Elgin, but I was charmed when I paid it a visit. And the surrounding country has been praised by those best qualified to appreciate natural scenery, at least better qualified than I am. By the Water Poet, 'the most pleasant and plentifull

country in all Scotland'; by Lugless Willie Lithgow, 'the delectable planure of Murry, a second Lombardy'; by John Macky, 'the Vale of Evesham is not comparable to it'. I could not have chosen a better place to be born ...'

The New Poly-Olbion (1967)

Editions of Young's *Collected Poems* appeared in 1950 and in 1960, and he is now recognised as belonging to the first order of modern nature poets. His poems are not 'about' nature: they explore the relationship between the natural world and the human world in intensely observed presentations of places, of seasons, and of all kinds of flora and fauna. He loved and often visited the landscape of his birth. Iain Crichton Smith, the Scottish poet and critic, speaks of finding a fresh, precious 'union of precision, wit, and strangeness' in his lyrics.

Andrew Young was honoured with an Honorary degree of LLD by the University of Edinburgh in 1951. The Royal Society of Literature conferred an honorary fellowship, and he received the Queen's medal for poetry in 1952.

Culbin Sands

Here lay a fair fat land;
But now its townships, kirks, graveyards
Beneath bald hills of sand
Lie buried deep as Babylonian shards.
But gales may blow again;
And like a sand-glass turned about
The hills in a dry rain
Will flow away and the old land look out;
And where now hedgehog delves

Andrew Young (1885–1971)

And conies hollow their long caves
Houses will build themselves
And tombstones rewrite names on dead men's graves.

Hard Frost

Frost called to water 'Halt!'
And crusted the moist snow with sparkling salt;
Brooks, their own bridges, stop,
And icicles in long stalactites drop,
And tench in water-holes
Lurk under gluey glass like fish in bowls.

In the hard-rutted lane
At every footstep breaks a brittle pane,
And tinkling trees ice-bound,
Changed into weeping willows, sweep the ground;
Dead boughs take root in ponds
And ferns on windows shoot their ghostly fronds.

But vainly the fierce frost
Interns poor fish, ranks trees in an armed host,
Hangs daggers from house-eaves,
And on the windows ferny ambush weaves;
In the long war grown warmer
The sun will strike him dead and strip his armour.

Ploughing in Mist

Pull the shoulder-sack
Close about his neck and back
He called out to his team
That stamped off dragging the weigh-beam;
And as he gripped the stilts and steered

They plunged in mist and disappeared,
Fading as fast away
They seemed on a long journey gone,
Not to return that day;
But while I waited on
The jingle of loose links I caught,
And suddenly on the hill-rise,
Pale phantoms of the mist at first,
Man and his horses burst
As though before my eyes
Creation had been wrought.

Suilven

It rose dark as a stack of peat
With mountains at its feet,
Till a bright flush of evening swept
And on to its high shoulder leapt
And Suilven, a great ruby, shone;
And though that evening light is dead,
The mountain in my mind burns on,
As though I were the foul toad, said
To bear a precious jewel in his head.

Mountain View

Can those small hills lying below
Be mountains that some hours ago
I gazed at from beneath?
Can such intense blue be the sea's
Or that long cloud the Hebrides?
Perhaps I prayed enough
By crawling up on hands and knees
The sharp loose screes,

Andrew Young (1885–1971)

Sweat dripping on the lichen's scurf,
And now in answer to my prayer
A vision is laid bare;
Or on that ledge, holding my breath,
I may have even slipped past Death.

Passing the Graveyard

I see you did not try to save,
The bouquet of white flowers I gave;
So fast they wither on your grave.
Why does it hurt the heart to think
Of that most bitter abrupt brink
Where the low-shouldered coffins sink.
These living bodies that we wear
So change by every seventh year
That in a new dress we appear;
Limbs, spongy brain and slogging heart,
No part remains the selfsame part;
Like streams they stay and still depart.
You slipped slow bodies in the past;
Then why should we be so aghast
You flung off the whole flesh at last?
Let him who loves you think instead
That like a woman who has wed
You undressed first and went to bed.

William J Grant (1886 – 1951)

Born in Advie, William Grant was a professional journalist and author. He was educated at Drainie School, near Lossiemouth – where Ramsay MacDonald was a pupil-teacher at the time – and at Robert Gordon's College, Aberdeen. He worked on local papers in the North-East before moving to Fleet Street, where he worked as a correspondent, mainly on agricultural matters, for a range of national papers. He then worked in India before being appointed Editor of the *Rangoon Times,* in 1922, a position he held for over ten years.

After retiring from professional journalism, he settled in London and wrote regular columns for the *Elgin Courant.* He often travelled to Moray. He published two novels, a collection of short stories (published by the *Elgin Courant*) entitled *Stories of Morayland*, and a study of India under the Raj, entitled *The Spirit of India.*

He died in London in 1951.

Archiestown
Strewn like grazing sheep
High on windy hill;
Grey as ancient keep,
Quiet and stark and still

William J Grant (1886 – 1951)

Is dun old Archiestown.
Winter's wrath is strong,
Grim his frosty stare;
Life is sad and long,
Making man despair
In dun old Archiestown.

Summer comes, however,
Blithely robed in light;
Then is man's endeavour
Brave from morn till night
In dun old Archiestown.

Elgin

Enchantment grips you, staid and dreamy town,
Whose loudest noise is but a lullaby
That lures the mumbling Lossie river down
To where the Moray woods are green and shy.
Your ancient facades turn their sternest face
'Gainst every change that rides the wings of time,
And credits all with noblest forms of grace
Whose slow and greying years are made sublime
By graven days of calm. This dun old Church
That spreads her godly breadth across your street
Expects the Milky Way to reel and lurch
If Friday's farmers come not to her feet,
And every child who plays on Lady Hill
To think of heaven as purer Bishopmill.

George Riddler (1886 – after 1937)

'RIDDLER, GEORGE No. 406221, Cpl. 6th Seaforths and RE.; born at Durris, Kincardineshire, 11th Feb., 1886, residing in Elgin for seven years; joined at Elgin, 6th August, 1914; served in France; prisoner of war from 22nd April, 1918; mentioned in despatches for Somme Offensive, July – August, 1916, and awarded M.M., 13th Nov., 1916. Son of James (deceased) and Christine Riddler, 38 Gilcomston Steps, Aberdeen. Occupation, house furnisher.'

Morayshire Roll of Honour, Elgin, 1921

This represents nearly all that we know about George Riddler. The 1911 Census shows him lodging at 72 North Street, Bishopmill, and working as a cabinet-maker. In 1921, he published, in Aberdeen, a book of verse entitled *51st Division Ditties* and, in 1937, a volume entitled *Ditties from the Veld*, from which *A Vision of Elgin* comes. The latter volume explores in verse the practical difficulties and the tensions of the pioneering life in South Africa. We must assume that he found some consolation in his memories of Moray.

George Riddler (1886 – after 1937)

A Vision of Elgin

As I sat and mused in my chair one night,
Free from the cares of the day,
I nodded and slept, then a vision so bright
Seemed to carry me far far away.

I was wafted far from the sun-scorched Rand
To a country so fresh and fair;
I stood once again on my own native land,
And oh, I was glad to be there!

I wandered again along green Lossie banks
As I oft did in days of yore,
With my dog behind playing all sorts of pranks
As each nook and crannie she'd explore.

And I climbed once again up steep Ladyhill
On the beauties of Elgin to gaze,
And I sighed as I looked on old Bishopmill
Then away to Birnie's green braes.

And I strolled once again in the old Oak Wood,
To Cuttie's Hillock I wended my way;
All nature seemed in accord with my mood,
The birds sang so blithely and gay.

As I gazed across the glorious Firth
To the hills so stately and grand,
I was awed at the beauty and hushed was my mirth
As I thought of the hills on the Rand.

Then to the Cloddach I wandered anew,
Where many a glad day I've spent,

Poetry of Moray

Camped there by the river with comrades so true
Under the old bell-tent.

But where are the comrades I used to know?
Scattered far over the world,
Hammered by fate and returning the blow
Wherever the Flag is unfurled.

But some, alas! I can ne'er again see,
They lie sleeping away there in France;
As I bowed my head to their memory,
I awoke with a start from my trance.

And as I sat up a dreary view
Of mine-dumps greeted my sight;
A wonderful work of man, it is true,
But hideous, how hideous to-night.

For the vision is fresh, and I want it so,
That vision of Elgin so fair;
In the days to come my thoughts will oft go
To the friendship and beauty that's there.

Hilton Brown

Hilton Brown was born in Elgin in 1890, the son of the Procurator Fiscal of Morayshire. He was educated at Elgin Academy and at the University of St Andrews, from where he graduated in 1910 with first class honours in classics. His career in the Indian Civil Service started soon after graduation, and continued until 1934. During the Second World War, he worked for the BBC as a producer in the Talks Department. He married Mary Gordon, originally from a Glenlivet family, in 1914. Their son, Leslie, became Director of Agriculture for Kenya and built an international reputation as an ornithologist.

Throughout his career, in India and afterwards, he wrote extensively, into the 1950s. He wrote several novels and short stories and literary biographies –notably of Kipling and Burns – and two well-respected books on British life in India. Three collections of poetry that were published between 1923 and 1935 contained many poems that had appeared first in magazines, notably in *Punch,* the highly popular weekly magazine that for many years carried the best humorous and satirical work of the day. He was a regular contributor to the *Northern Scot Christmas Number.*

Throughout his long sojourn in India, and on many other travels, Hilton Brown's verses turned constantly to his home in Moray. He died in Nairobi in 1971.

Poetry of Moray

The Good House (Covesea, Morayshire)

A house by the sea
Looking over to Ross,
A dyke and a tree
And a braeside of moss,
A cliff and a beach,
The surf and the spray
And the long sea-reach
Over Cromarty way.

A house with a view
From the Ord to the Main
And the far-away blue
Beyond Brora and Tain;
Morven waist-deep
In his lowlier kin
And Clebrig asleep
At the back of Loch Shin.

If the gods were inclined
To send gifts to the good,
If fortune were kind
And we lived where we should,
It would maybe hold me,
It would maybe hold you
That house by the sea,
That house with a view.

Glen, a Sheepdog

I ken there isna a p'int in yer heid,
I ken that ye're auld an ill,
An the dogs ye focht in yer day are deid,
An I doot that ye've focht yer fill;

Ye're the dourest deevil in Lothian land,
But, man, the hert o ye's simply grand;
Ye're done an doited, but gie's yer hand
An we'll thole ye a whilie still.
A daft-like character aye ye've been
Sin the day I brocht ye hame,
When I bocht ye doon on the Caddens green,
An gied ye a guid Scots name;
Ye've spiled the sheep an ye've chased the stirk,
An rabbits was mair tae yer mind nor work,
An ye've left i the morn an stopped till mirk,
But I've keepit ye a' the same.
Mebbe ye're failin, an mebbe I'm weak,
An there's younger dogs tae fee,
But I doot that a new freen's ill tae seek,
An I'm thinkin I'll let them be;
Ye've whiles been richt whaur I've thocht wrang,
Ye've liked me weel an ye've liked me lang,
An when there's ane o us got tae gang –
May the guid Lord mak it me.

The Convent Garden

The convent stands on the Indian hills
With a smiling face to a sunlit south
And a singing river that swirls and spills
Over the ghats to the lowland drouth;
Out on the plains the colours harden
From gold to ochre, from blue to grey;
But it's green and soft in the convent garden,
Any hour of the day.
The convent garden's a haunt of peace,
For it's set in a land where peace was born,
Where the clouds sail over like silver fleece –

Rosy at evening, opal at dawn;
A land where the great hills, softly wooded,
Whisper that all good things endure,
Shining at noon, at night cloud-hooded,
Comforting, kind, secure.
Here in the garden the nuns will sit,
Their eyes to the south and their thoughts to home,
And homeward their varying fancies flit –
To Brussels or Paris, Florence or Rome;
And sun and cloud and the shadow-races
Magic the known familiar view
To visions of old, remembered places
These wandering fancies knew.
For Mother Cecilia the Apennines,
And the little towns of good St Francis;
For Sister Marie, olives and vines,
And the Cote d'Azur, where the heat-haze dances;
For Mother Antony, brown as a berry
With long, long years of the suns of Hind,
A moment's glimpse of the crags of Kerry,
A breath of the Galway wind.

Mother Cecilia's been toiling here
Since her last home leave in nineteen-five;
Sister Marie's beginning to fear
She'll never go back to Provence alive;
And Mother Antony keeps on thinking,
'This year – next –,' but there's work to do,
And Ireland's sinking, sinking, sinking
Into the westward blue.
But memory's pleasant and dreaming's sweet,
And it's warm and quiet by the convent wall,
And each is glad of the garden seat

And the comforting view that serves for all –
Where subtle colour and deft engraving,
Slants of sun and shadows astir,
Picture for each what her eyes are craving –
The land that was home to her.

Spey
'The Lang Run o Spey' – Morayshire Proverb

I am Spey;
Where Corryarrick on high
Looks over Lochy and Ness
And the west wind comes weeping;
Where the rain clouds lift and press
And the hill mist thickens and thins,
And by red gully and grey
The young burns go leaping, leaping
There cradled am I,
And the Lang Run begins.

Shouting and strong and bold,
By Garva and Crunachan, Laggan and Cluny I come
Black as night in the shade,
In the sun a glimmer of gold;
Like a war horse loosed to the fray,
Clad and caparisoned, frantic for bugle and drum,
Eager and gay;
Till out of a fold
In the hills where the red deer run
Truim leaps with the flash of a well-used blade,
And we that were two are one.

Then, speed! speed!
A rush and race by Ruthven and Farr,
Where Feshie falls like a mist from Mar,
A rush and a race by crag and birk,
By farm and forest, by cot and kirk;
Faster and faster – coursing, leaping,
Swelling, thundering, conquering, sweeping
Till, by all the Badenoch hills that bore me,
My own dear Strath lies fair before me!
Then who is the monarch of rivers, say?
Who, indeed?
Who of them all but Spey?

Who loves my Strath?
That haven set in the hills,
Where the wild winds' wrath
Is tempered a while and stills
Its voice to quiet weather?
Where Spring comes down the path
Gold starred with daffodils,
And Autumn lingers long in the purple heather?
In all broad Scotland hath,
Match me the gallant land
Twixt Nethy and Aberlour,
Kings' castle, minstrels' bower,
Highland and howe together,
Stronghold of Spey in his power
Spey with a lilt in his heart, a sword in his hand!

A long run and a good;
But the end draws near.
Down by the Orton wood,
Down, down to Fochabers,

Till the scrannel sea-fowl shear
Through the beating air that stirs
With the loud sea's neighbourhood,
And the Firth lies open and clear.
Full-grown in majesty,
Crested and plumed and splendid,
Swift as the running deer,
Spey comes safe to sea;
The Lang Run's ended!

Ella Gilbert (1890 – 1975)

Ella Gilbert was born and brought up in Lossiemouth, the daughter of Edward Gilbert and his wife, Elspet Edwards. She had two brothers, Edward and Alexander Grant Gilbert. Edward joined his father in the family joinery business. In the First World War, Grant was awarded a Distinguished Conduct Medal at Beaumont Hamel in 1916. Later, he emigrated to Kenya as a missionary. He died in 1944 of complications following an inoculation for yellow fever. Ella, meanwhile, qualified as a school teacher, stayed at Rowan Brae in Stotfield with her parents and brother, Edward, and spent her teaching career in the Primary Department of Lossiemouth Junior Secondary School.

Her poems deal with her world: the teaching of children, the sea and the shore, Lossiemouth, and what she knows of love. They are conventional and smoothly finished and they can use the language of Ella Gilbert's home town with real conviction. Her best-known piece is *Greengoon*, which tells the tale of the mythical witch that lives on the Skerries off the West Beach and which has been used for many years to frighten naughty children. Ella Gilbert's work was published in the *Northern Scot* and in newspapers and magazines across Scotland. Her poems were published in two volumes, *Spindrift* (1932) and *Ae Forenicht* (1960).

Ella Gilbert (1890 – 1975)

Nickum Days

The day was sunny, warm an fair,
The sky was blue as sky could be,
The call o sun an win an air
Was added tae the call o sea.
'Twas jist a day o days abune,
Ower gweed tae spen wi slate an buik,
Half dizzen nickums there an then
Made up their minds that they wad juke.

Sae doon the schule dyke side they gaed,
Doon tae the quarry at the wast,
An lauchin laich at their ain ploy,
Their bags intil a fin bush cast,
Syne skirtin roon the heich north dyke,
The loons as ane took tae their heels.
Here Ding-dong got a glisk o them,
An swift pursued th' escapin chiels.

Noo ower the Coulard hill they sped,
The langest legit set the pace,
As barfit, lichtly cled they ran.
Puir Ding-dong peched as he gave chase,
'Lowse a' yer claes, loons,' cried the first.
'We're daeint,' cried the ither five,
'An e'er we're thrashed for jukin schule
We'll hae a dook, an sweem an dive.'

Aye lauchin, swiftly on they sped,
Doon by the mines, an ower the stanes.
Though taes were stubbed an shins were barked
There wer'na ony broken banes.
They cuist their claes an carried on

Intae the Hythe up tae the neck,
Till turnin shoreward in their sweem,
Their merriment got sudden check.

For Ding-dong, large as life, they saw,
An grinnin sour – his was the joke.
He'd got their claes aa in a bing,
An sittin guard by't, had a smoke.
The consternation wasna mowse,
'Twas noo beyond a lauchin matter
As lang as Ding-dong had the claes
The loons jist be t'bide in t' water.

The game looked lost. The loons mous fell,
Foo tae git oot was noo the cry,
Wi Ding-dong sittin by the claes,
Till aa at aince quick-witted Sye
Cried, 'Loons, mak for the divin pole,
An splash an dive aroon tae fool 'im,
He'll niver notice there's ane less,
An I'll jink roon the rock an bool 'im'.

Aul Ding-dong smokit quietly on,
Watchin the loons, nor did he guess
That in the bourrach o bobbin heids
There was ae curly reid ane less.
Till – fat was that? – a stane? – noo, twa?
A shooer took Ding-dong in the rear,
An comin oonexpeckit like,
Pat's bonnie plans aa oot o gear.

As Ding-dong raize tae face the fae,
That hurled stanes fae the shelterin rock,

Ella Gilbert (1890 – 1975)

He turned his back, an in the nick
The claes war taen by watchin Jock.
Their object gained, they warna laith
T'lat Ding-dong ken the game he'd lost.
But he'd Authority on his side,
The loons had time tae coont the cost.

An authority maun be upheld, ye ken,
An discipline's rules maun be maintained.
Tho the loons had haen ae glorious day
Fine kent that they'd a lickin gained.
Neist day the mester raxed for's tag,
Tae pey the price there was nae shirkin,
An he looked fu stern, but, in spite o't aa,
He'd quhauve tae keep the wicks o's mou fae workin.

The Sea an the Soun o't

It's a sair quhauve tryin tae sleep,
Fan ye canna fa awa.
In simmer it's the heat;
In winter it's the snaw.
But it's hantle waur than either
Fan ye are far awa
Fae the sea, an the soun o't.

I've tried tae sleep on Deeside,
An up the side o Don,
An in the hert o Perthshire
But niver sleep cam on.
For the silence there fair deaved me;
I was listenin, even on,
For the sea, an the soun o't.

Neath the roar o city traffic
I hae tried tae trace the soun
O the ripplin waves aa lauchin
On a simmer efternune.
Though the din gaed on oondauchelt,
My ear was aa atune
Tae the sea, an the soun o't.

An fan I gang my last lang road
Gin ye be left ahin,
Will ye see til't that I tak my rest
Far fae the city's din?
I'll sleep there like a little un
Till the Dawn come glowin in
By the sea, an the soun o't.

The Grey Nor-East
Foo div they ca't the grey Nor-East?
Fat div they mean by grey,
Liken they't tae the grim, gaunt beast
That prowls at the close o day?

Or div they likent tae honoured eild
That stotters wi shoothers bent,
Wha's hoary heid wi its siller hair
Is the sign o a life near spent?

Tae them is the grey o the birk on the brae,
An the grey o the lichened scaur,
An the grey smirr o rain on the hill
The same as dead ashes are?

Ella Gilbert (1890 – 1975)

Or is it the grey o her winter sky
As it girns ower her grumlie sea,
That gars them think the Nor-East,
Is as grey tae the hert as the ee?

Little they ken the real Nor-East
Wha only see the grey,
For the fire that glows at the hert o her
Is the kind that burns for aye.

As the Spartan mither in aulden times
Her sons tae endurance trained,
The Nor-East does sic like an hantle mair
For the love that she niver hained,

Binds her sons tae her wi siccar ties
Tae the uttermost ens o the earth,
An they loe till the hinner end the grey Nor-East,
The mither that gave them birth.

A Little Learnin

The lassie was new at the teachin,
An the mester, that he could tell
Fat progress the bairns were makin
Took the class for a lesson himsel.

Noo, the littl'uns werena lang entered,
They were learnin book English tae speak,
So the mester decided to question them
On the names o the days o the week.

An fat is the day? He spiered them.
The bairns answered him that.

An fat is the morn, fat yesterday?
Again the answers cam pat.

An fat was the day afore that?
A laddie answered some dour,
Sae the mester, tae liven him up, said,
Noo, laddie, o that are ye sure?

But the mester had bairns o his ain,
Sae gaed oot wi his tongue in his cheek,
Fan the loonie, fair dumfoonert, spiert,
'Div ye nae ken the days o the week?'

Greengoon

Did ye iver hear o Greengoon?
Her hame was on the Skerries.
She lived on drablicks, dulse, an wulks,
An labsters' blue-black berries.

An, woman-like, she decked hersel –
She wore a seaweed wreath
Upon her theck o ropy hair,
She'd muckle airn teeth.

Her hans war cleeks tae clim the rocks,
Her feet war shapeless dauds,
Her goon, green tangle blades an slake
Wad scunnert earthly jauds.

Aroon her throat a necklace was
O fish een set in rows,
Her airn teeth was sharp an bricht
Aneth her beakit nose.

Ella Gilbert (1890 – 1975)

Her een, foo can I tell o them?
Wide open, like her mou,
Wi neither lids nor lashes there,
Wad look ye through an through.

Her goon at throat an waist an breist
Was snodly held in place
Wi crossin lines o limpit shalls,
An shalls grew on her face.

An John-o-Groats an caufie's mous
Grew thick among her hair.
She couldna scrat ye wi her nails,
For she had nane tae pare.

An mony a nyatterin bairn grew gweed
At 'See, here's Greengoon come.
She'll grip ye wi her lang bress cleeks
An hyeuk ye up the lum!'

Twa Proposals

Jock spiered me the ither week,
Pressed the pint wi aa his micht.
I said, 'Na,' an as ye'll see,
Daein sae, did fat was richt.

For he spak nae word o love,
Telt me o his routh o gear,
O his hoose, an lans, an beas,
Even tae the auld grey mear.

An I listened tae his list –
'Twas like a displenish sale.

Did he think tae win me thus,
As I quhauve sair for ma kale.

Fan at last he stopped, I said,
'Gin ye'd gowd, ay by the pail,
Wantin love I wadna wed.
An – ma hert is nae for sale.'

Syne cam Rab. He's young an puir,
In his pooch is scarce a plack.
An his wealth o this warl's gear
Is the claes upon his back.

'Lassie, I hae loed ye aye.
Love for you I canna tine.
I hae nocht but youth an health.
Lassie, will ye nae be mine?'

I said, 'Ay.' Fat could I say.
Love for me was jist the ae thing.
As ma hert was nae for sale,
I hae gient tae him, for naething.

We hae love, an youth, an health.
Gin we're spared, will work for plenty.
There are bigger things than wealth;
Life's afore's at ane an twenty.

Margaret Winefride Simpson
(1893 – 1972)

Margaret Winefride Simpson was born in Buckie in 1893. As the only child of a prosperous couple – her father was a banker – she received a privileged education on the continent. The family moved to Friars House, Institution Road, Elgin. In the years following the First World War, she devoted herself to charitable works. She helped to found the Elgin branch of An Comunn Gaidhealach; formed and trained an orchestra and choir; and became an ardent Scottish Nationalist

Between 1923 and the end of her life she published ten volumes of verse and innumerable individual and occasional poems that regularly appeared in publications from the *Times Literary Supplement* and *The Manchester Guardian* to the *Press and Journal*, the *Scots Magazine* and the annual *Magazine of The London Morayshire Club*. For forty years, her work was ever-present in the *Northern Scot Christmas Number*.

She was technically skilled and her best work reveals a sure and delicate lyrical touch and an excellent ear. Her best work is probably in Scots – a feeling expressed by Compton Mackenzie in his introduction to her collection, *Day's End* (1929). There are strong devotional and patriotic thrusts to her verse. There also emerges an intense love for Moray – for its landscape and its folk and the changing faces of its seasons. Her work may now be regarded as being essentially nostalgic and of minor interest, but there can be no doubt about her technical and linguistic skills nor of her serious and scholarly approach to her craft. Several of her volumes include translations into Scots of poems from Gaelic, French, Italian, Spanish, German and Portuguese. She is buried in St Ninian's Churchyard, Enzie.

Villanelle

O winter wind, lat grievin be,
Lat grievin be, and murn nae mair:
Simmer sall set thy sorrow free.

New hurt the heavy hert sall dree;
Thy weariness awa sall wear:
O winter wind, lat grievin be.

Wi aa the waes the warld sall see
What wae hast thou that can compare?
Simmer sall set thy sorrow free,

Yet what delicht sall puirtith pree
When time sall solace thy despair?
O winter wind, lat grievin be.

What fear onkent can trouble thee,
What misery that nane can share?
Simmer sall set thy sorrow free,

But man in dule doth live and dee;
A birn mair brief is thine to bear:
O winter wind, lat grievin be:
Simmer sall set thy sorrow free!

Margaret Winefride Simpson (1893 – 1972)

The Waukrife Win

The waukrife win gangs back an fore
Thro the teem, mirk haas o Nicht,
An the blinterin starnies winner an glower,
Wae at the sorrowfu sicht –
For lang sall he watch or he sees oot-bye
The grey face o Daylicht:

An lang sall he wait or he hears the Dawn
Come tirlin at the pin…
Troth, there's little content when a cankert carle
Is neither to haud nor bin,
An the heich, back waas o Midnicht dirl
Wi the wail o the waukrife win!

Rhyme for Two

O it's ae wish for Winter
Whase hert is hard an cauld,
But anither wish for Simmer
When aa the flooers unfauld!

Ae thocht for the snawdrift
That lingers on the hill,
But anither for the sunlicht
When the haughs lie warm an still!

It's ae wish for the feck o fowk
The hale wide warld through,
Ae thocht aye for aa the lave,
But anither thocht for you!

For the true hert has a treasure
But twa can haud or hain,

An the leal hert has a secret
That's shared by nane but ane:

Sae it's ae wish for the feck o fowk
The hale wide warld through,
Ae thocht aye for aa the lave,
But anither thocht for you!

Lilianne Grant Rich (1910-1997)

Lilianne Green was born in Glenlivet and brought up on Speyside at Tulchan and Pitchroy. She attended school at Advie and in Aberlour and went on to train as a teacher in Aberdeen. After she married, she and her husband lived in Sevenoaks, Kent, and spent many years abroad, mainly in South Africa. She was widowed in her early fifties. Thereafter, settled in Aberdeen, she spent much of her time travelling all over the world on cruise ships.

She published four books of verse – *The White Rose of Druminnor* (1969), *Echo of Many Voices* (1980), *The Horn Speen* (1983) and *The Pink Rose of Chenonceaux* (1988). She wrote extensive reminiscences about her early years on Speyside, many of which were published in the *Northern Scot Christmas Number*. The prose tends to be sentimental and self-congratulatory; in her verse, she sometimes finds an effective economy of language and form.

The Other One
Ane gat his money an his gear:
She gat his body strong and braw;
She gat his gowden wedding ring-
But his hert she never heild at aa.

Though nichts he's taen her in his airms
Fin darkness happ'd wi blessed wing,
Anither lass aye lies atween
Wi hair as gowd's the wedding ring.

At kirk, at wark, in buiks, in lear,
In drink he ettles tae forget,
But the image cherished in his hert,
The lass he tint – she binds him yet.

Second Threshold

Jist lay yer hans in mine
An naething say,
Though fegs it's mony a spate
That's gushed
Sin yon ill day
Fin you an me
Broke tryst
An took oor seprate way.

Say muckle tae explain!
Routh o life's storms
Throu years we sinner spent
In fremmit airms –
Aa by;
An noo we've met,
Nae menseless wastefu wishin
Nae regret –
Jist tak my hans in yours;
Wi benedictions lay
Yer urgent mou on mine
An naething say.

Lilianne Grant Rich (1910 –1997)

Journey into The Past

The Music Hall wi folk wis steerin! Dyod!
It wis the Christmas Fair for next year's Mod!
Gaelic 'A Hundred Thousand Welcomes' said;
Tables wi glitterin merchandise were spread.
I did my bit o purchasin and syne,
My basket fu, thinks I, 'I'll mak for hame.'
But, edgin roon, I spied a muckle neep
As big's my heid – it only cost 5p,
A michty bargain for an OAP.
I humpt it oot, and up oor street ca'ed Union,
Hopin it widna rowe on someane's bunion.
Up fifty steps wi mony a pech and grunt
(Nae elevator in this tenement),
Syne dirdit doon, and gazed upon my prize,
'If spared,' says I, 'the morn I'll hae neep brose.'
Oh, the gran yoam that filled my hoose neist day!
The windows rinnin doon wi condensation –
My mou, like Pavlov's dog, wi anticipation-
I was a bairn again on fair Strathspey!
Odours evocative turn back the clock:
Time disappears; doors in the past unlock;
Fifty years fled as if they'd never been
And I wis aince again a teenage quean!
Floatin aboot me mon the kitchen steam.
Dear folk I'd loved took shape as in a dream
That neep brose wis a feast o celebration
As folk lang gane ca'ed in for the occasion.
I bocht a neep – a mundane thing you'd gauge?
But, Oh! It brocht my magic pilgrimage!

Jessie Kesson (1916 – 1994)

Jessie Kesson is the most celebrated author associated with Moray in modern times. Information about her early life is sketchy. She was born illegitimate at the Workhouse in Inverness to Elizabeth MacDonald, a member of a large farming family, originally of the Alves-Mosstowie area. Jessie's father was John Smith, woodcutter, widower (41), of Redbog, Orton, which happened to be the address of Jessie's grandparents.

In the early years she and her mother lived in the Elgin area, staying sometimes in the Model Lodging House. Jessie attended at least four different schools. Elizabeth (Liz) MacDonald's life was one of desperate poverty, small-time prostitution, and dependence on alcohol. She neglected Jessie who, at the age of ten, was admitted to Proctor's Orphan Training home at Skene, Aberdeenshire. She stayed there until she was sixteen. At Skene School, she met the Dominie who fostered her skills and her need to write. After working as a 'kitchie deem', Jessie suffered a major breakdown and spent a year in the Mental Hospital in Aberdeen. While recovering at Abriachan, above Loch Ness, in 1937, she met and married Johnny Kesson.

Through the 1940s, the Kessons lived on a variety of farms across the North-East, before settling in the Elgin area, first at Coulardbank, then at Wester Calcots, then at Linksfield, on the northern edge of Elgin. During this time, she wrote exten-

Jessie Kesson (1916 – 1994)

sively for the *Elgin Courant*, for the *Scots Magazine*, and for the BBC. It is estimated that she had over one hundred radio plays broadcast in the course of her career. Her work won the praise of such writers as Neil Gunn and Nan Shepherd.

In 1951, with their two children, the Kessons left for London. Johnny worked on the roads; Jessie's work ranged from cinema cleaner to Care Assistant to life model to producer on BBC *Woman's Hour*. *The White Bird Passes*, based on her childhood experiences in Elgin and Skene, was published in 1958 to enthusiastic reviews. *Glitter of Mica* (1963) and *Another Time, Another Place* (1983) followed. The latter was made into a successful film. Money worries eased. She received Honorary Doctorates: from Dundee University and from the University of Aberdeen – thus acquiring, in her seventies, the Scarlet Goon she covets in the poem below.

Moray was always important to Jessie. After moving to London, she maintained contact, through letters and visits, with a wide range of old friends and neighbours.

Throughout her adult life, Jessie was writing. She wrote novels, stories and radio plays and a handful of fine poems. She strove, in her writing, to come to terms with the difficulties of her own childhood and the privations and insecurities of cottar life. Her works are short, intense, harrowing, often tragic. She worked at all times to achieve what she called 'the sma perfect'. *Blaeberry Wood*, the earliest poem we have, was published in the *Scots Magazine*, in 1942; *The Spell-Binders* was written in 1984.

In Autumn 1994, Johnny died. Jessie died of lung cancer less than two months later.

Blaeberry Wood

Our Street had a face I did not know, in the early
>   morning light –
Not tired and hot and crowded, as it had looked last night.
I came upon it unawares,
Before the day, with pressing cares,
And noise and dust and weary heat,
Unceasing tramp of hurrying feet,
Had caught it up. Night must have lent some magic
>   to Our Street.
And deep in me arose an eagerness
That I must dance to show my happiness.
But there was never an eye to see
This fun and gaiety of me.
Yet I knew someone understood.
'Twas all because of Blaeberry Wood.
Down our Close, up Murdoch's Wynd,
I left the East-end far behind,
And now must walk with quiet feet
Along West Road – the rich folks' Street,
With villas standing stiff and prim,
Each with its garden neat and trim.
They all seemed very much the same
But for a number or a name.
And yet their dust-bins in a row
Made my heart beat, my eyes to glow.
How carefully I'd search each bin,
Excited, plunging headlong in
For a broken doll or a coloured tin.
Sometimes a dog would come as well,
And prowl around, and smell and smell.
Wagging his tail, to the next he'd run,
As if he, too, found dust-bins fun.

Jessie Kesson (1916 – 1994)

Life at the child must often smile –
The rich folks' dust-bins a Treasure Isle!
And now the long straight country road
With my dust-bin booty for my load.
Here was the wood. Within I flew
To a secret spot that alone I knew,
Where hyacinths, wild and wet and blue
In their hundreds and hundreds grew.
There on the wet grass, on my knees,
I pressed my face in the heart of these.
No smell I know is half so good
As the hyacinth tang in a morning wood.
I ever saw them with new eyes.
My heart was quick to meet surprise.
So now I set to work with a will.
'I think my pail will never fill.'
The rustling trees and the rising wind;
The town's left ever so far behind.
And the crackling twigs, and the bird-calls shrill;
The wood was never a moment still.
And now the droning of a bee.
Everything's busy round here – but me.
I just watch and watch the hole by the tree
For the rabbit that I was never to see.
The sun grows warm. The moss is deep.
I'd like to sink – and to sleep and sleep.
It's colder now. I think I'll call;
The world is strange when the shadows fall.
I'm not afraid, afraid at all;
But, all the same, I think I'll call.
Now where's my doll and flowers and tin?
What can I carry the whole of them in?
If I but could, if I but could,

I'd have carried away the half of the wood
Home in my arms. The foxgloves broken,
The hyacinths limp, are just a token.
Every bit of me is blue.
Hands, face, and knees, too.
But my heart has a vivid colour I know.
It's so warm inside me – a fire aglow.
So-long! So-long! It's been a treat.
On my way again with hurrying feet,
Half-glad, half-sad, back to Our Street.
I'll never grow too old to love Surprise,
Thank God! I still can see through a bairn's eyes.
A bygone trip, an enchanted wood –
A little girl who understood.

A Scarlet Goon

O the regret as a body growes auld!
I wad hae likit a scarlet goon
an a desk o my ain 'neath the auld, grey Croon.
But I nivir wun nearer the College airts
than a Sunday walk doon the cobbled toon.
King's gaithered aa its ain wise thochts
intae its ain grey fauld.
Bein young, I grippit on tae the daftest thocht of aa,
feel, feckless, wi naething to ponder on
but a tryst tae be keepit by Brig o Don.
Gin I'd hae worn a scarlet goon
Fat wad I ken?
Mair or less than I ken noo
livin mang men wha nivir heard o
Aristotle, or Boyle, that made a law,
or Pythagoras, an sic like chields
wha's wisdom's gie heich up, and far awa.

Jessie Kesson (1916 – 1994)

My Alma Mater's jist the size o aa the fowk I ken,
An jist the colour o their thochts,
grey whiles wi mole-hill griefs that mak true mountains;
gowd harled wi sma lauchs and greater humour;
black wi humphy-backed despair;
alowe wi hopes that whiles come true
but mair than often find slow beerial there.
And whiles it's green,
For jealousy torments even lads
wi nae letter ahint their names.
Aa that I ken.
– But still, I'd hae likit a scarlet goon,
an a desk o my ain 'neath the auld grey Croon,
Learnin a little from the wise.
Dancin wi gowden sheen,
Lauchin wi care-free eyes,
– Instead o liftin tatties in mornins glaured and cauld.
– O the regret as a body growes auld!

Fir Wud

Here for lang
a yalla yitie quatens
the warld's steer an mortal thochts
wi the lift o's sang
Like velvet atween ma hot bare taes
the fir-loam sifts
birstlin things cleave tae ma claes
an the foosty guff o an ancient wud
drifts ower an bye
If foriver in this wud I just could lie
an tine ma thochts
an sniff the resin loam-filled air
an watch the queer wud dirt gaither tae battle

ower ma hair
Sharpenin draughts nip roon ma face
Nivir sae wide awak, I shut ma een
Syne, like a lustful quine,
Gie aa masel tae the wud's embrace.

The Spell-Binders

I miss the ancient mariners
the tellers of tall tales
who clustered round the close mouth
of my childhood
and cornered me
reluctant to set but one believer free
I miss the sound of – Verily!
The vows that proved it so
As sure as Death
As God's my Judge
May I drop Dead
the ebb and flow
and tides of talk receding in their sighs
You're far owre young to ken
the way it was –
the things that happened –
then
Yet!
Youth was no impediment,
'twas then I knew
a tale is still a tale
be it false or true.

Bibliography

Sources of poems included in this volume:

Holland, Richard: *The Houlate*, Bannatyne Manuscript (1881)
Robertson, James: *The Buke o the Howlat* (2017)
Alves, Robert: *Poems* (1782
Cock, James: *Hamespun Lays: or simple strains of an unlettered muse* (1820)
Jamieson, Robert: *Popular Ballads and* Songs: *2 Volumes* (1806)
Grant, John: *The Penny Wedding* (1836)
Milne, John: *The Songs and Poems of John Milne of Glenlivat* (1871)
Hay, William: *The Lintie o Moray* (1851)
Murdoch, James: *The Autobiography and Poems of James Murdoch, known as 'Cutler Jamie'* (1863)
Tester, William Hay Leith: *Selected Poems of La Teste* (1887) and ten other volumes, published between 1865 and 1890
Sutherland, Frank: *Sunny Memories of Morayland* (1883)
Middleton, Lady Eliza Maria: *Ballads* (1878); *Alastair Bhan Comyn* (1889)
Donaldson, William: *The Martyr Queen; and other poems* (1867)

McQueen, James: *Beauties of Morayland* (1895);
   The Minstrel of Moray (1895); *Lays of Findhornside*
   (1911); *A Fiddler's Philosophy* (1914)
Wellwood, James: *Poems* (1920)
Mackenzie, David J: *Poems* (1920)
Dawson, May C: *Tinkers Twa in Peace and War*
   (Gardner, 1925?)
Symon, Mary: *Deveron Days* (Wyllie, 1933)
Wells, Nannie Katharin: *Twentieth Century
   Mother and other poems* (1952)
Caie, JM: *The Kindly North* (Wyllie, 1934); *Twixt
   Hills and Sea* (Wyllie, 1939)
Young, Andrew: *Collected Poems* (Hart Davis, 1950;
   Selected Poems (Carcanet, 1998)
Grant, William J: *Poems* (1940)
Riddler, George: *Ditties from the Veld* (1937)
Brown, Hilton: *Both Sides of Suez* (Noel Douglas, 1930);
   The Gold and the Grey (1936)
Gilbert, Ella: *Spindrift* (Stockwell, 1932); *Ae
   Forenicht* (1960)
Simpson, Margaret Winefride: *Day's End* (Gardner, 1929)
Rich, Lillian Grant: *The White Rose of Druminnor*
   (Aberdeen UP, 1969); T*he Horn Speen* (1983)
Kesson, Jessie: *Somewhere Beyond*, ed Isobel Murray
   (Black and White, 2000)

Some other works consulted

Alison, James: *Poetry of Northeast Scotland*
   (Heinemann, 1976)
Alves, Robert: *Sketches of the History of Literature* (1796)
Bawcutt, P and Riddy, F: *Longer Scottish Poems*
   (Scottish Academic Press (1987)
Bennett, Susan et al: *Women of Moray* (Luath, 2012)

Bibliography

Blair, Kirsty: *Poets of the People's Journal* (ASLS, 2016)
Douglas, Robert: *Sons of Moray* (Elgin, 1930); *Lays and Legends of Moray* (Elgin, 1939)
Edwards, DH: *Modern Scottish Poets* (Brechin, 15 volumes between 1880 and 1897)
Geddie, John, ed: *Old Morayshire Characters* (Elgin, 1931)
Hewitt, David: *Northern Visions* (Tuckwell, 2001)
Hewitt and Spiller: *Literature of the North* (Aberdeen UP, 1983)
Lowbury, Edward and Young, Alison: *To Shirk no Idleness. A Critical Biography of the poet Andrew Young* (Univ. Salzburg, 1997)
MacMillan, D and Byrne, M: *Modern Scottish Women Poets* (Canongate, 2005)
Murray, Isobel: *Jessie Kesson: Writing her Life* (Kennedy and Boyd, 2000/2011)
Rampini, Charles: *Moray and Nairn – County Histories* (Blackwood, 1897)
Warner, Graham N: *The Muse in Morayland* (Elgin, 1933)
Wheeler, Leslie: *Ten Northeast Poets* (Aberdeen UP 1895)
Young, Andrew: *The Poet and the Landscape* (Hart Davis, 1962); *The New Poly-Olbion* (Hart Davis, 1967)

Glossary

antrin – occasional
arles – reward
bajan – first year student at Aberdeen University
beets – boots
biel(d) – shelter
birn – burden
birze – squeeze
bruik – dirt
buss – bush
but-the-hoose – kitchen
cankert – ill-natured
carritch – Catechism
caukit – sharpened (of horseshoes)
chaulder – measure (of grain, usually)
chiel – fellow
clarty /clorty – messy
clyack – end of harvest
congou – tea
conach'd – destroyed
corbie – crow
cronach – coronach, lament
croose – smart
cutter – whisky flask

Glossary

darg (n) – work
deavin – nagging
devaal (n) – cease
dhubrack – sea-trout
ding – strike, drive
droon – drown
duddies – clothes
dweeble – feebleness
Eel-even – Hognamay
eident – diligent
ettle – intend
ern – alder
fa – who
fan – when
files – whiles
foo/fu – how
faur – where
fairlies/ferlies – wonders
farl – oatcake
feck – majority, bulk
fidgin fain – showing uncontrolled joy
fir – fir 'candles' from the peat-bog
fleg – frighten
flype – turn inside out
forcey – vigorous
forenicht – evening
forhooiet – abandoned
fremmit – different, strange, unfamiliar
fulp(ie) – whelp
fun – found
gairach – coalfish
gait – road
gar/gaur (v) – cause

Poetry of Moray

geats – children
ged – pike (fish)
girnal – meal-chest
gradden – coarse oatmeal
grieve – farm foreman
groff-write – child's handwriting
grue (v) – shudder
gyte – daft
halfling – farm boy
hammel – humble, home-made
hannie – little hand
happit – covered
hirples – stumbles
houch – hough, thigh
howdie – midwife
ilk/ilka – each
jurram – chorus (of a rowing song, originally)
kaies – jackdaws
kaig – keg
knock – clock
kayak – cake
lauchin – laughing
levin – lightning
litted – dyed
leal – loyal, faithful
loan (n) – lane
loon – boy
lowse – stop work for the day
lug – ear
Mahoun – the devil
marra – equal
mensefu – wise, sensible
menseless – stupid, wrong-headed

Glossary

men't – mended
moo /mou – mouth
moulets – gulls
mullie – snuff-box
muntins– mountings
murlacks – crumbs
nae mous – imposing
neeper/neiper – fellow-workman (neighbour)
oondauchelt – unabated
pairis – parish
pandrop – type of mint sweet
pech – pant
pints – laces
plenishin (n) – furnishing
pyock – pouch, bag
quean/quine – girl
queet – ankle
queetikins – leggings
rax – strain
reist – rest
ruck – stack
sanshach – cocky
sareless – without taste
sark – shirt
sauch – willow
seenil – seldom
seggs – rushes, sedges
shaavin – sowing
sheemach – matted
shilt/shelt – pony
shouther – shoulder
sinner – separate, apart
skailin – dispersing

skreich o day – first light
skyte – drop
slungs – slings
soosht – washed
soss/soce – mess
spiel/speel – climb
steek – close, shut up
sternies – stars
steeve – thick, firm (of food)
stew – dust
stilpert – lanky
stirk – bullock
stouf – clod-hopper
sumph – booby, simpleton
ted – youngster
teem/toom – empty
ticht – tight
tine/tint – lose/ lost
tow – twine
trackies – tracts
trappin - ribbons
trig – neat, trim
trow – trust
tweddle – a public dancing occasion
tyaave/quhauve – struggle
uncos – unusual bits of news
wahnie – fishing rod
wale – pick
walloch (v) – dance
walshach – dreariness
wame/wyme – belly
wanworth – worthless
waukrife – sleepless

Glossary

win oot – go outside
winnock – window
wud – (1) wood; (2) mad
wyte – fault
yaavins – barley chaff
yalla yitie – yellow-hammer
yoke – set to work
yoky – itchy

Selected Glossary for The Book of the Howlat

alkyn – of every kind
berne –men (poetic)
bill – scroll
ble – colour
blist barne – blessed child/bairn
breid – breadth
browdin – adorned
brusit – embroidered
bysyn – monster
cais – jackdaws
cheverand – shivering
chydand – complaining
cliftis – cliffs, steep banks
deir – deer
dicht – treat (me)
dow – dove, a term of approval
dyte – write, written work
endurand – during
fairhed – beauty
fallowe – fellow
fangan – catcher
feid – hostility

Selected Glossary for The Book of the Howlat

feir – friend
gryntar – granary-keeper
gyde – gown
houris – canonical hours
huf – stay still
laik – river
le – sheltered
leid – one, a person
lende – stay
levar – the better (thing to do)
lowne – calm
mendis – remedies
mold – the ground, earth
mufe – proceed
neb – beak
nevyn – name
nok – hook
persevantis – heraldic officers
pikmawis – black-headed gulls
prunyeand – preening
pyotis – magpies
raikit – wandered
rane – rigmarole
rerd – howl
rocatis – smocks
ruf – repose
ryiue – tear
savoruss – sweet-smelling/tasting
scarth – cormorant
sentence – subject matter
suowchand – rustling
swar – neck
swyth – swiftly

trast – trust
trowis – truce, peace
Ternway – Darnaway
waike – weak
weir – fear, confusion
wryth – turn, cast
wyte – blame

About the Editor

Richard Bennett was born and brought up in Moray and educated at Elgin Academy and at the University of Aberdeen. He started his career as an English teacher in Dundee before moving to Milne's High School, Fochabers, and later to Elgin Academy.

Buy our books online or follow us at:

www.speybooks.co.uk
fb.me/speybooks

Also available from Spey Books

The Summer Crew
John Bennett

The Summer Crew is a novel set in the late 1980s on the salmon netting at the mouth of the River Spey. Follow the exploits of Sandy Geddes, the crew and the various poachers, politicians, ravers, TV presenters, clergymen and aristocrats who cross their path.

'A must for your library,' **Dr Robbie Shepherd MBE**
"9/10 - Scottish Book of the Week,' **Dundee Courier**
'The Para Handy of the East Coast,' **The Sunday Post**

Buy The Summer Crew at:

www.speybooks.co.uk

'Speak weel o the Hielands, but bide in the Laich.'

Old Morayshire saying